The Backyard *playground*

Recreational Landscapes & Play Structures

CREATIVE PUBLISHING international

CHANHASSEN, MINNESOTA

www.creativepub.com

Credits

Executive Editor: Bryan Trandem
Creative Director: Tim Himsel
Managing Editor: Michelle Skudlarek
Editorial Director: Jerri Farris

Lead Writer: Brett Martin
Additional Writers & Editors: Barbara Harold,
   Karen Ruth, Dane Smith
Technical Editors: Randy Austin, Philip Schmidt
Copy Editor: Tracy Stanley
Lead Art Director: Kari Johnston
Senior Art Director: David Schelitzche
Illustrators: Jan-Willem Boer, Wayne Jeske,
   Jon Simpson, Earl Slack
Photo Stylists: Herb Schnabel, Joanne Wawra
Stock Photo Editor: Julie Caruso

Director, Production Services &
   Photography: Kim Gerber
Production Manager: Helga Thielen
Studio Services Manager: Jeanette
   Moss McCurdy
Photo Team Leader: Tate Carlson
Additional Photographer: Andrea Rugg
Scene Shop Carpenters: Justin Austin,
   Greg Wallace

Copyright© 2003
Creative Publishing international, Inc.
18705 Lake Drive East
Chanhassen, MN 55317-
1-800-328-3895
www.creativepub.com

Printed on American Paper by:
   R.R. Donnelley
10 9 8 7 6 5 4 3 2

President/CEO: Michael Eleftheriou
Vice President/Publisher: Linda Ball
Vice President/Retail Sales & Marketing: Kevin Haas

THE BACKYARD PLAYGROUND
Created by: The Editors of Creative
Publishing international, Inc. in cooperation
with Black & Decker. Black & Decker is a
trademark of the Black & Decker Corporation
and is used under license.

Library of Congress
Cataloging-in-Publication Data

The backyard playground : recreational
landscapes & play structures.
      p. cm. -- (Black & Decker outdoor home)
Includes index.
ISBN 1-58923-059-0
1. Children's playhouses--Design and construc-
tion--Amateurs' manuals. 2. Playgrounds--
Design and construction--Amateurs' manuals.
3. Garden structures--Design and construction--
Amateurs' manuals. 4. Landscape construction--
Amateurs' manuals. 5. Family recreation--
Amateurs' manuals. I. Creative Publishing
international. II. Series.

TH4967.B33 2003
690'.90--dc21   2002041765

Contents

Introduction

We all know that children love to play. What's more, they *need* to play. Play lets them learn privately from their mistakes and progress at their own pace. In play, they can make their own rules and ignore "real" time. Play also helps foster a child's physical, emotional, social, and intellectual development. Most importantly, play is just plain *fun*.

This book is about children having fun! *Your* children. What better gift could you give them than exciting new places to play? You and your children can work together to create a backyard that matches their interests.

Why plop down the old standby pre-fabricated swing set in the grass when you can do something much more creative? *The Backyard Playground* gives you great ideas for designing and planning play areas that will keep your children entertained and engaged for years to come. Plus, the book shows you how to build play areas for children of all ages.

You'll learn how to choose play structures, projects, and landscaping to enhance your play area. Since each child has different ideas of what's fun, you'll also find out how to make your backyard playground suit your children's interests.

In *The Backyard Playground* you'll find projects to build now, whatever the age of your children, and some options for future projects. The best play area offers a wide variety of activities and levels of challenge for children as they grow. This book has plenty of ideas for all ability levels.

You may want a few permanent play pieces and a few that can be moved from place to place across your yard. *The Backyard Playground* has plans for

both permanent structures and movable items. You may decide to dismantle and store some equipment during certain seasons or while waiting for younger siblings to "grow into" them and this is possible with many of the projects.

This book includes information on the safe placement of play areas. It also describes ways projects can be adapted as children grow up. For example, a sandbox can become a raised flower bed and a play house can become a storage shed after the children have outgrown it.

Before you start planning your projects, check local codes to learn of any restrictions on the placement of playground equipment, including any size limitations or visibility requirements from the street or road. Also, be sure to talk to your insurance agent about the equipment you are including in your backyard. Make sure your policy protects you from liability in the event someone is injured on your playground.

A special play area in a child's own backyard is extra fun. With all the tips and plans in this book, it will be easy to create that special place.

Choosing Play Activities

How do you go about choosing play equipment for your child or children? What is an appropriate play structure for a seven year-old? How can play areas be personalized? The following pages can help answer these questions and more. Here are brief, informative sections on what kids like to do, and how those activities fall into the four types of play. There's also information on what sizes and types of play structures are appropriate for different ages. Suggestions are given for adding personal touches to your play areas, along with some pointers on supervision.

What Kids Like to Do

The first thing you notice about children at play is that they test their physical limits. Even babies are constantly reaching and stretching with their arms and legs. Soon they add crawling to their list of skills, then climbing, then walking....

Kids become even more active as they refine their motor skills. Climbing, running, and throwing become the primary activities. Structures with multiple levels, from simple slides to complex play equipment, are popular for climbing. If you provide some open grassy spaces, children will naturally create activities that involve running and throwing. As the ability to balance is gained, hopping and jumping are new skills to learn and practice. Children love to hop and leap over things on the ground—sometimes even other playmates. As they explore new heights, children take up the challenge (or dare!) of jumping to the ground.

Performing each of these physical feats is satisfying, and children soon combine and experiment with them. For instance, hopping without falling quickly becomes hopping or jumping from higher and higher elevations without falling. Running soon needs to be running faster. Simple throwing evolves into throwing farther and with more accuracy. With these activities, kids can sometimes push their boundaries, and a parent's patience, to the limit.

Most children go through a phase of wanting to build or manipulate items. At early stages, it may be simply stacking small blocks or arranging and rearranging a group of toys. Later, the structures become larger and more extravagant, often with more detailed planning. Making sand sculptures or designing a tiny town with streets and buildings can hold a child's attention for hours.

As they broaden their physical abilities, children become more confident and begin to explore their world. The outdoors offers a uniquely rich environment for new activities. Play spaces don't have to be large, but they must be inviting and interesting. You'll be amazed at the discoveries your children make—a seed sprouting, a squirrel eating a nut, or birds bathing—and how excited they'll be to share them with you.

Along with focusing on their own physical skills, children begin to socialize with others. Some children develop an interim activity between playing alone and playing with others by secretly observing the others. A "hidden" space where a child feels secure can help him or her gain confidence for this new type of play. Many children use such a hideaway simply to have some time alone to play quietly, read a book or magazine, or just to think.

When children are ready to play with others, activities may take the form of organized games with rules. The structure can be loose, such as a game of tag, or the structure can be defined, such as a sport like baseball. These games are perfect opportunities to make friends as well as to show off new physical skills.

Types of Play

Types of play activities vary among children, changing to reflect a child's age, interests, and surroundings. Child psychologists divide play into four components: physical, social, imaginative, and intellectual. Though any given activity may include all four types of play, it is useful to look at each separately to make sure your play area encourages all four.

Physical activity is probably the most common type of play. It's certainly

one of the first images that comes to mind regarding children and play. Physical play is an important part of a child's development. Running, jumping, and climbing help strengthen muscles and improve dexterity. Play areas should foster physical activity in a safe, stimulating, and age-appropriate manner.

Another important component of play is social interaction. Social interaction can take many forms on the playground. It can be children pushing each other on swings, playing games such as tag, or sharing toys in the sandbox. Children develop communication skills by learning to lead, follow, and share in a group. These social interactions encourage each child's development and give him or her a sense of belonging. Children test their confidence by assuming the role of leader and setting rules. Conversely, there are opportunities to follow a leader's directions and share equipment. This often involves emotions—learning to express them and control them.

Using the imagination is another aspect of play. Kids are constantly using their imaginations during play, pretending their swing is an airplane, the climbing wall is the side of a steep mountain, and the fort is a pirate's secret hideaway. A group of children can imagine together as part of a game, such as making believe they are police officers or fire fighters, or individually, such dreaming of being a famous movie star or pop singer.

A component of play, intellectual activity, is integral to each of the other three and commonly takes the form of problem solving. There are many kinds of challenges to overcome and problems to solve in any physical, social, or imaginative play situation. This can include working with building blocks, making arrangements in the sandbox, or manipulating the movable components of a play structure, such as games and puzzles that are built into activity panels.

Children sometimes seem to focus on one type of play at a time. One child may excel at physical activities—a star athlete in the making? Another may truly love to role play—will Broadway beckon? Yet another child becomes immersed in reading—a brilliant writer blossoming?

Just as children appear to become immersed in one type of activity, their need for variety pops out and their whole mix changes, sometimes suddenly and without warning. Those interests usually change again and again on the path toward adulthood.

Matching Play Areas to Children

Children will have more fun and play more safely if they are using age-appropriate equipment. Kids develop in stages, so a playground designed for a 10-year-old will be different from one designed for a 2-year-old. Child psychologists who study play behavior have developed lists of activities and determined the age at which a child generally becomes interested in each one. To help you choose among the projects in this book, we have made some general age-appropriate suggestions to use as guidelines. Many manufacturers of playground equipment also suggest age and size ranges for the children who use their products.

The three general age groups for most playground equipment are 2 and under; 2 to 5; and 5 to 12 years of age. Each age group is separated by differences in size, ability, and coordination, so your play structures should be geared toward the ages of the children who will be using it.

For very young children, different textures and contrasts in color can stimulate the senses. Because they are still crawling or just learning to master the skill of walking, crawling areas, handles to pull themselves up on, and small ramps are appropriate.

Children in the second age group enjoy crawl tunnels, multiple access platforms, tables for sand and water, spring rocker equipment, activity panels, swings, small slides, and playhouses. As a safety precaution, most equipment designed for children under the age of 5 sits lower to the ground to lessen the impact of falls.

Play areas for 5 to 12 year-olds typically include rope or chain climbers, horizontal bars, merry-go-rounds, see-saws, slides and sliding poles, tire swings, open

spaces to run and play, and semi-enclosed structures to encourage fantasy play and socializing.

If your child has physical limitations, a stimulating and fun play area might include creating transfer stations to reach raised platforms and wide pathways to accommodate a wheelchair. Your child's physical therapist or special education professional can recommend appropriately challenging play areas.

The most important criteria for choosing an activity is whether or not your child is ready to participate in it. You need to take into consideration your child's age, size, and developmental level. There are no hard-and-fast rules to follow. Decisions about play space are, in the end, your best guesses.

Kids like to do things they've already mastered—it reinforces their sense of confidence and gives them comfort. They also like to try things that are new—it challenges them and provides a sense of accomplishment when they conquer it. The best play areas offer both kinds of activities. You can usually add accessories onto existing play structures, as well as bring new items into the playground to keep kids engaged as their needs and interests change. The goal of planning a playground is to create an area that is safe, stimulating, and meets the changing needs of your children.

AGE APPROPRIATE PLAYGROUND ACTIVITIES

Ages 2 & Under: Small ramps or stairs; crawling areas; infant mazes; learning walls; small tunnels; toddler swings; and play handles for pulling themselves up.

Ages 2 to 5: Balance beams; low platforms with multiple ramp and ladder access; tables for sand, water and manipulation of materials; tricycle paths with various textures; play steering wheels; flexible spring rockers; sandboxes; slides not taller than 48"; activity panels; swings; playhouses; observation stations; bridges; planter boxes; and forts.

Ages 5 to 12: Rope or chain climbing walls; horizontal bars; tire swings; merry-go-rounds; sliding poles; spiral slides; monkey bars; track gliders; see-saws; putting greens; bird houses; water slides; wide open spaces; gym rings; basketball courts; garden carts; tree houses; and retreats.

Personal Touches

One of the most important aspects of creating a play area is encouraging your children to participate in the planning and design process. When your children feel involved in decisions concerning the playground, they will enjoy it even more. In addition to asking their advice on what to include, make them part of decisions such as color selections for playground equipment and the types of flowers to plant in the garden.

Since this is an area for children, it should be something they feel comfortable with. The structures should be inviting and challenging, rather than intimidating or boring. Allowing your children to add personal touches to the playground, such as putting their handprints in the path leading to the play area or helping paint the picnic table or playhouse, can make all the difference in the world. Kids are full of ideas. Even if they're not all practical, implementing some of them allows your kids to feel a sense of ownership.

When your backyard playground stimulates your children's imagination and encourages them to play outside, then you've done a great job. By following the advice in this book, you can't miss!

Supervision

At every age, children need supervision when playing on playgrounds, even the playground in your own backyard. As a parent, your role is to nurture and encourage positive emotional development by observing, supervising, and facilitating play without interfering.

The type, frequency, and duration of interaction with the parent will vary with each child and the particular type of activity. You can participate and supervise in your children's activities without seeming intrusive. For younger kids, this is easy because their primary attachment is to you. They demand almost constant attention and want to show off their latest feats. They want you to catch them at the bottom of the slide or push them on a swing. Interaction with older children can include playing catch or practicing free throws on the basketball court.

As children get older, they prefer less and less oversight. Some structures, such as forts and play houses, allow children to play with relatively little supervision since they are mostly enclosed. You and your child can negotiate how much "private time" is appropriate for the play structures in your backyard. This private time is important because when children are alone in their play areas, they often participate in role playing where they imitate family members, especially adults. They copy a person's speech or mannerisms. They may even fabricate dramatic performances. While this type of play tends to be quieter and less physical, it offers all the same socialization components as sports. It gives children an opportunity to act out fantasies and dreams.

Landscaping for Playgrounds

Most people don't immediately think of landscaping when they think of backyard playgrounds, but it's an important component of a safe, enjoyable, and attractive play area.

This section contains information on choosing a play site, options for year-round play, borders and dividers, pathways, steps, and children's retreats.

Play Sites

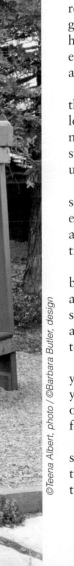

The size and type of your yard will, to a large extent, dictate what you can include in your backyard playground. In a small yard you may have to carefully maximize use of space, but even a large yard requires careful site planning.

Choosing the perfect site for your playground requires a good deal of thought. When selecting a location, keep in mind what else is in your yard and plan accordingly. For example, don't put a slide or climbing wall right behind your flower garden unless you want kids to trample through it. For safety's sake keep the play area away from any driveways or roadways. Also make sure the play area maintains a safe distance from obstacles such as fences, hard surfaces, and structures that could cause injury (for more on safety, see pages 26 to 27).

You want your children playing in an area that you can easily monitor from your house, deck, or porch. You need to keep the play structure at least 6 to 36", maybe even more, from your property lines to meet most zoning requirements. Keep structures well away from above-ground utility lines. And before siting your playground, have all local utility companies identify water, gas, and electric lines running through your property so you can avoid building over them.

Because the defined squares of typical urban yards are the most restrictive, you'll have to be creative if you want lots of equipment or extensive landscaping. With planning, however, it is possible to put in a playhouse, fort or swing set. Combining structures, like placing a sandbox under the clubhouse, is an efficient use of limited space.

Suburban yards typically include some type of landscaping, maybe a flower garden, fence, or hillside that can enhance the visual appeal of the play area. You can build a large play structure and still have room for other activities, such as basketball, croquet, or volleyball.

In a rural yard, you'll probably have ample space to build the structures of your choice and include as many accessories as you want. You can have a tree house, a swing set with slide and climbing wall, and a sandbox in addition to open spaces for a putting green or picnic table to accommodate children of all age groups.

Pathways and stepping stones can be part of any size yard and playground. Landscaping can be used directly in your play structures, such as using a tree for a tree house, or indirectly, like a row of shrubs that serves as a border for the play space.

As with other features of the playground, landscaping should be fun. Every yard can include a variety of colors through the use of different plants, dividers, berms, and the like.

©Teena Albert, photo / ©Barbara Butler, design

15

Year-round Play

After building your backyard playground, you'll want your children to enjoy it—all year long. If you're fortunate enough to live in a location that offers temperate weather year-round, your children may be able to use your outdoor play area for most of the year. For everyone else, using the playground during the depths of winter or the peak of summer is more of a challenge.

There are some simple things you can do to ensure that your children enjoy

their play equipment during all four seasons, such as selecting an appropriate location in your backyard and choosing items that are portable. Of course not every component of your playground should be movable, but do include some items that can be brought indoors during severe months. Obviously, tree houses and swing sets are too big to move, but balance beams, garden carts, planter boxes, and putting greens are all projects that will keep your children entertained in any season.

When considering which play items are best suited for year-round play for your kids, think about how the projects can be used in each season rather than focusing exclusively on any one time of the year. If you live in an area with a rainy, but not cold, winter, the same roof or tenting that provides summer shade can also provide winter rain protections. Blustery fall or spring winds can be tamed by using fencing or shrubbery as wind breaks to make the play area more comfortable. In areas with cold and snowy winters, make sure play structures won't interfere with sledding hills or potential ice skating rinks.

©Mark Gibson

In most areas, selecting a location that is at least partially shaded is important for keeping cool and limiting exposure to the sun. On a hot day, it can be as much as 20° cooler in the shade than in direct sunlight. Direct sunlight can make metal components of the play structure extremely hot, which could result in burns. Pick a convenient spot under large deciduous trees, if possible. Since deciduous trees drop their leaves in the winter, they allow winter sunlight to warm play areas. Evergreen trees create shade year-round and they also drip sticky sap, so they are not as desirable. If you don't have trees large enough to provide shade, consider using tarps, tenting, or umbrellas to shelter the play areas. Include windows or open areas in playhouses, forts, and tree houses to allow breezes to circulate fresh air.

Borders & Dividers

Fences, gates, trellises, hedges, and walls can add to the attractiveness of your yard while improving the safety, security, privacy and climate of your play area. If you already have borders or dividers in your backyard, consider how the play areas will be affected by these plants and structures.

Borders and dividers can add stimulating visual backdrops to a play area. Using bold colors or unusual textures makes them fun and appealing for kids.

A nice aspect of most borders and dividers is how easily they can be changed. You can plant new flowers, shrubs, or trees to increase a border's density or remove plants for a sparser look. A fresh coat of paint and different decorative features can be used to periodically change the children's area as they mature.

Borders and dividers serve as more than visual props for a playground. They provide safety barriers between your children and the outside world. Fences or hedgerows can set perimeters for play areas. As children start to explore their environment and test their strength by running or by playing games such as hide-and-seek, they tend to push their limits further and further. A physical border sets firm boundaries and can keep children from wandering away from their designated play space. Keep your play structures a safe distance from borders and dividers so they don't pose hazards to children while they're playing. Since borders and dividers are part of the play area, eliminate sharp edges or toxic plants and substances.

Enclosing the playground with a fence or shrubs also ensures privacy for your children as they play. Just as borders and dividers keep your kids in your yard, they keep other people and stray animals out. A simple fence can prevent a neighborhood child from entering your yard, using your equipment, and possibly getting hurt. A fence or wall helps protect you from liability issues, which is why swimming pools are required to have fences around them.

Fences, walls, and trellises, especially those covered with vines or plants, can create effective sound barriers. Buffering

©Michael Gilmanis, photo / ©Barbara Butler, design

the enthusiastic screaming and other loud noises generated by playing kids can keep them from disturbing your neighbors. As you know, it's almost impossible for children to play quietly. Sound barriers also reduce outside noises, such as traffic. This is particularly beneficial for homes located near busy streets or noisy highways.

The right type of fence or trellis can also provide a defense against some elements of Mother Nature. For example, hedges, staggered board fences, and trellises block the wind by breaking strong gusts into small, harmless eddies. Solid fences, on the other hand, offer little help because the wind surges up and over them, then shoots sharply downward in swirling gusts. If you live in a windy location, select a fence or other outdoor walls that will buffer your playground from the wind.

With a little planning, you can create borders and dividers that will enhance your play area in many ways.

©Nordicphotos.com

Pathways & Steps

Pathways and steps are another important part of the landscaping for your backyard playground. Pathways and steps add decorative touches while preserving your lawn and adding additional play space.

You can have a lot of fun creating interesting pathways and steps for the playground. As with other areas of the playground, this is something your children can help create. In fact, one of the nicest features of pathways and steps is that you can easily personalize them. When making paths or stepping stones out of concrete, inscribe your children's names and birthdays, or include meaningful designs. Your children can participate in the project by making their hand or foot prints in the concrete. In addition to different textures and colors, you can use a variety of patterns and shapes to construct the paths and steps.

Pathways and steps allow you to direct the course children follow to and from

©Teena Albert, photo / ©Barbara Butler, design

their play spaces. Children can walk or run from the house to the playground along a prescribed route rather than tromping through your flower garden or wearing a path in the grass. Contrasting colors and textures, as well as personal designs, give paths and steps an inviting, stimulating look that allows children to start playtime as soon as they step outside.

Stepping stones are a creative option for directing children to the playground. Stepping stones invite kids to follow them to the play structure. The stones can be spaced at whatever intervals you choose and children will naturally jump or hop from stone to stone. Stepping stones are also easier to move and relocate than most pathways. If you set the stepping stones into the ground so only the top surface is exposed, you can easily mow over them.

Games such as hopscotch and tic-tac-toe can be easily built into a path leading to the playground, giving children extra opportunities for imaginative play. Paths and steps also provide hard surfaces for sitting, playing board games such as checkers, and playing with toys that work better on a flat, level surface, such as race cars.

Even a simple concrete sidewalk can be dressed up and turned into an accessory for play. Outdoor chalk allows children to write on concrete, draw pictures, and invent new games. The most convenient feature of all is that the chalk can be easily washed away with water.

Since this is a children's playground, there's really no way you can go wrong. If you like it and your kids like, then it's a success.

Children's Retreats

Just as important as offering plenty of room for children to play and run around is providing an area for them to seek solitude. Spending time alone is a necessary part of childhood development, allowing children to think, dream, read books, use their imaginations, and enjoy themselves without any distractions.

While tree houses, forts, and playhouses can offer children safe havens, kids sometimes prefer areas that are uniquely their own rather than sharing common spaces. Many children will create their own retreats using their natural surroundings. A retreat can be as simple as a crevice at the foot of a favorite tree or a spot in a dip in the yard. They can also be more involved, such as a lean-to fort of tree branches propped up against the side of the garage or fence, or a hideout under trees or tall flowers.

You can include elements in your backyard that will encourage a retreat theme. Building a bench or chair in a corner of the lawn, behind some shrubs or a few trees, gives children the beginnings of a sanctuary.

Planting sunflowers, vines, lilac bushes, or other tall plants and shrubs also creates retreat possibilities. Plants provide foliage to obscure the area, at least in part, from the rest of the yard. Children enjoy making tunnels between bushes, under shrubs, and through undergrowth.

Children often use the shrubs and vines to create their own canopies and houses. Imagination and ingenuity enable them to build individual spaces that suit their own tastes and personalities. Just be sure you choose child friendly plants. Stay away from anything that's thorny, may cause allergies or rashes, or is likely to produce splinters.

Almost anything that shields a child from the rest of the world can become part of a retreat, given just a little effort and creativity. Start with what you have. Look around your yard for spaces or structures that could become a retreat. Have your children help you imagine the possibilities.

Large Play Projects

Considering the declining fitness level of children, parents need to do all they can to encourage their kids to engage in active, imaginative, and stimulating play. The play structures in this section help kids develop dexterity and work their large muscle groups. This type of play builds the basis for physical activity for the rest of children's lives.

This chapter is filled with project plans. It also includes specific instructions for some of the more complex aspects of building your backyard playground projects, such as digging and pouring footings, setting posts, constructing stairs, and building rails.

Playground Structures

The projects detailed in this section are large structures that children of every age will enjoy. Your children and their friends are sure to spend countless hours playing in and around these structures.

Because these projects are large and nearly permanent, you will want to plan their placement carefully. Lay rope or hose on the ground to mark the "footprint" of each project. Be sure to include the safety surface dimensions from page 27 when figuring these measurements. To find out how solid surface structures will change your view or affect sight lines, use poles, ropes and tarps to create a temporary structure the same dimensions as the project. Taking the time to study the structure's placement will increase your overall satisfaction with the project's outcome.

The structures in this chapter are primarily constructed with lumber, including some pressure-treated lumber. Treated lumber, also called pressure-treated lumber, is typically used where play structures come into contact with the ground, since it provides long-term protection against rot, decay, and termites. Due to recent concerns about the safety hazards of the chromated copper arsenate (CCA) that was used to treat lumber, arsenic treated lumber will not be available for residential use after December 31, 2003. Instead, lumber will be treated with other preservatives, such as alkaline copper quat (ACQ), copper azole types A and B (CBA-A and CA-B), and sodium borates (SBX). When buying treated lumber, check with your lumberyard or home improvement store representative to make sure it doesn't contain arsenic.

While the new breed of treated lumber is deemed less hazardous, it's also more corrosive to steel than CCA. Therefore, when working with treated lumber, make sure to use nails, fasteners, and fittings that are hot-dipped galvanized or stainless steel. When working with any type of treated lumber, always wear gloves, avoid breathing the sawdust, and don't burn the scrap wood. When the structure is finished, apply a coating to exposed surfaces on a regular basis to keep it sealed. It's important to use treated lumber as called for in the plans in this section. Untreated wood may only last a year or two when in contact with moisture, including the ground, whereas treated lumber can last decades.

Before starting any large project, check with your local building department to see if a building permit is required and if any restrictions are applicable to your project. You may need to set your play structure back a certain distance from your property lines and keep the structure below a specified height.

Safety

Safety, of course, is paramount to enjoying your backyard playground. In addition to establishing rules for using your playground and providing adequate supervision, you can make your play area safe by observing some basic rules when building it.

Drive the nails and set the screws completely into the wood so the heads are flush with the surfaces. Nails or screws that stick out of the wood can pose a serious risk to children as they run, swing, slide, and play on the equipment. When you're finished building your project, examine it for nails or screws that are popping out. Also check for nails or screws that have gone completely through boards and are sticking out the other side. If that happens, clip the end off or grind it down flush with the board.

Countersink holes for anchor bolts so the heads and nuts are recessed. Crimp hooks with pliers so sharp edges are not exposed. Apply a wood preservative or paint to wood structures to help protect against splinters and preserve the lumber.

If you plan to build more than one play structure, keep at least nine feet of space between them. Securely mount the structures or anchor them to the ground. The projects in this section are secured in a variety of ways. The children's play structure is staked into the ground, the playhouse is mounted on a wood skid foundation, the fort posts are set 48" into the ground, the arbor is fastened to concrete footings, the clubhouse is secured by the sand in the sandbox, and the A-frame swing set is fastened with auger anchors.

Conduct regular inspections of the structures and look for unusual wear and tear, loose boards or connections, and loose rails. As children bring their toys and belongings into the play structure, make sure they are placed in areas that don't pose a hazard. Teach children to keep toys away from the top and bottom of stairs and ladders.

Safe Surfaces

One of the keys to a safe playground is having a surface that cushions your children when they fall. Falls account for approximately three-quarters of all playground injuries, according to the U.S. Consumer Products Safety Commission. Including a safe surface, therefore, is an important part of your play area.

Stay away from hard surfaces, such as asphalt, concrete, dirt, and grass. Some of the more common loose-fill materials you can use for your playground include:

Wood mulch: Wood mulch is essentially wood that has been chopped into small pieces by a wood chipper. It is available by the truckload or can be purchased by the bag.

Wood chips: Wood chips are small pieces of wood, twigs and leaves of similar sizes that have been through a wood chipper. The chips come from tree limbs, branches, and brush. It is also readily available.

Engineered wood fibers: This material is uniformly sized shredded hardwood fibers.

Sand: Both fine sand and coarse sand can be used for playground surfaces. Sand is fairly inexpensive, however, it's easily displaced and gets in children's clothing.

Pea gravel: Pea gravel is small round pieces of washed gravel, generally less than ⅜" in diameter. Gravel is less likely to attract animals than sand or wood. The disadvantage is that gravel can freeze together and become hard in freezing temperatures.

Shredded tires: Shredded tires are just that: shredded tires. They have superior shock absorbing qualities and will not deteriorate over time. Be sure to use shredded tires that do not contain wire from steel belted tires and that have been treated to keep them from discoloring clothing.

Each of these surfaces is relatively easy to install in a play area. Apply the material you choose to a depth of 12" and extend it at least 70" in all directions from the play equipment for maximum protection against falls. For swings, the surface should extend to a distance twice the height of the swings both in front and in back of each swing. If you have an 8' swing, for instance, cushion a surface that extends 16' in front and in back of the swing.

You'll either need to build a retaining barrier or dig a pit to contain the surface material. The area should have good drainage so the material doesn't sit in water. Most surfaces need periodic maintenance, such as grading or adding more material to keep an adequate depth.

Wood mulch

Wood chips

Engineered wood fibers

Sand

Pea gravel

Shredded tires

Tools & Materials

Power auger or
clamshell posthole digger
Tape measure
Pruning saw
Shovel
Reciprocating saw or handsaw
Torpedo level
Hoe
Trowel
Plumb bob
Utility knife
8" concrete tube forms
Portland cement
Sand
Gravel
J-bolts
Wheelbarrow
Scrap 2 × 4

Footings

Concrete footings hold posts in place and support the weight of playground structures. Check your local codes to determine the size and depth of footings required for your area. In cold climates footings must be deeper than the soil frost line.

To help protect posts from water damage, each footing should be poured so it sits 2" above ground level. Tube-shaped forms allow you to set the depth of the footings and extend the top of the footings above ground level.

It is easy and inexpensive to mix your own concrete by combining portland cement, sand, gravel, and water. You can mix your concrete in a mixing box or a wheelbarrow.

Before digging, consult local utilities for the location of any underground electrical, telephone, gas or water lines that might interfere with footings.

HOW TO DIG & POUR POST FOOTINGS

Step A: Dig the Footings & Insert the Tube Forms

1. Dig holes for post footings using a clamshell digger or a power auger. Center the holes on the layout stakes. For holes deeper than 35", use a power auger.

2. Measure the hole depth using a tape measure. Local building codes specify the depth of footings. Cut away tree roots, if necessary.

3. Pour 2 to 3" of loose gravel into the bottom of each footing hole to provide

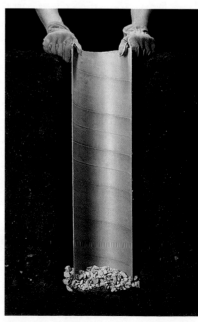

A. *Insert tube forms into the footing holes, leaving about 2" of tube above ground level.*

drainage under the concrete footings.

4. Add 2" to the hole depth (so footings will be above ground level) and cut the concrete tube forms to that measurement using a reciprocating saw or handsaw. Make sure the cut is straight.

5. Insert the tubes into the footing holes, leaving about 2" of tube above ground level. Use a level to make sure the tops of the tubes are level.

6. Pack soil around the tubes to hold them in place.

Step B: Mix & Pour the Concrete

1. Mix dry ingredients for concrete in a wheelbarrow or a mixing box using a hoe.

2. Form a hollow in the center of the dry concrete mixture. Slowly pour a small amount of water into the hollow. Blend in the dry mixture using a hoe. Add more water gradually, mixing thoroughly until the concrete is firm enough to hold its shape when sliced with a trowel.

3. Pour the concrete slowly into the tube forms. Carry it from the wheelbarrow or mixing box using a shovel. Use a long stick to tamp the concrete, eliminating any air gaps in the footing.

4. Level the concrete by pulling a 2 × 4 slowly across the top of the tube form, using a sawing motion. Add concrete to any low spots as necessary.

5. Retie the mason's strings on the batter boards and recheck the measurements.

Step C: Insert the J-bolt into the Concrete

1. Insert a J-bolt at an angle into the wet concrete at the center of the footing. Lower the J-bolt slowly, wiggling it slightly to eliminate any air gaps.

2. Set the J-bolt so ¾" to 1" is exposed above the concrete. Brush away any wet concrete on the bolt threads.

Step D: Position the J-bolt

1. Use a plumb bob to make sure the J-bolt is positioned in the exact center of the post location.

2. Make sure the J-bolt is perfectly plumb using a torpedo level. If necessary, adjust the bolt and repack the concrete. Once the concrete has hardened, cut away the exposed portion of the tube using a utility knife.

B. *Fill the forms with concrete. Use a long stick to tamp the concrete.*

C. *Insert a J-bolt at an angle into the wet concrete at the center of the footing.*

D. *Use a torpedo level to make sure the J-bolt is plumb. If necessary, adjust the bolt and repack the concrete.*

Tools & Materials

Framing square
Ratchet wrench
Tape measure
Reciprocating saw or circular saw
Hammer
Screwgun
Level
Combination square
Metal post anchors
Nuts for J-bolts
Lumber for posts
10d or 16d joist hanger nails
2" deck screws
Long, straight 2 × 4
1 × 4 lumber
2 × 2 stakes

Posts

Posts support beams and transfer the weight of the play structures to the concrete footings or the ground. For maximum strength, the posts must be perfectly plumb. The procedures for setting round posts and square posts are the same.

To prevent rot or insect damage, use treated lumber for posts and make sure the factory-treated end faces down. Using treated lumber is especially important for the fort project where the posts actually sit in holes in the ground.

Metal post anchors are used to attach posts to concrete footings. They have drainage holes and pedestals that raise the ends of the wood posts above the concrete footings so they don't sit in water. Follow the manufacturer's specifications to determine specific nail size. When concrete footings are not used, the posts can sit on top of the ground, as in the clubhouse project, or in the ground, as called for when building the fort. Regardless of how the posts are mounted, they must be plumb.

HOW TO SET POSTS

Step A: Install Post Anchors

1. Place a long, straight 2 × 4 flat across two or three concrete footings with one edge tight against the J-bolts. Draw a reference line across each concrete footing, using the edge of the 2 × 4 as a guide. Remove the 2 × 4.

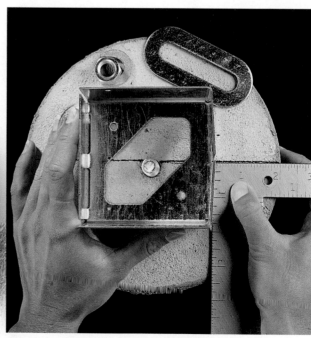

A. *Use a framing square to make sure the post anchor is positioned square to the reference line drawn on the footing.*

Remove the 2 × 4.

2. Place a metal post anchor on each concrete footing, centering it over the J-bolt. Use a framing square to make sure the post anchor is positioned square to the reference line drawn on the footing.

3. Thread a nut over each J-bolt, and tighten it securely with a ratchet wrench.

Note: This step is only required when using concrete footings.

Step B: Set the Posts

1. Use the elevation drawings from your plans to determine the height of each post. Add 6" for a cutting margin, then cut the posts using a circular saw or reciprocating saw. For large posts, you may want to use a handsaw. Make sure the factory-treated ends of the posts are square. If necessary, trim the posts to square the ends.

2. When using concrete footings, set the post in the anchor. Tack it in place using a single 10d or 16d joist hanger nail. When not using footings, set the post in the hole on top of 2 to 3" of gravel.

Step C: Brace the Posts

1. To brace the posts, place a 1 × 4 flat across the post so it crosses the post at about a 45° angle approximately halfway up the post. Attach the brace to the post using a single 2" deck screw.

2. Drive a pointed 2 × 2 stake into the ground next to the end of the brace. Use a level to make sure the post is plumb, adjusting the post as necessary. Attach the brace to the stake using two 2" deck screws.

3. Plumb and brace the post on the side perpendicular to the first brace using the same method.

4. Secure the post to the post anchor using the manufacturer's specified nail size, typically 10d or 16d galvanized nails. Some anchors require using lag screws as well. When the posts are placed in the ground rather than a footing, backfill the hole with soil, packing the soil tightly around the post using a board or rake handle.

B. *Place each post in an anchor and tack into place using a single 10d joist hanger nail.*

C. *Plumb and brace the post on perpendicular sides.*

Stairs

The goal of any stairway is to allow people to move easily and safely from one level to another. The stairs described in this book allow children to access their play structures.

Building stairs requires four calculations. The number of steps depends on the vertical drop. The vertical drop is the distance from the surface of the deck to the ground. Rise is the vertical space between treads. Building codes require that the rise measurement be about 7" for decks. However, since these projects are geared toward children, the treads tend to be closer together. Run is the depth of the treads. A convenient way to build playground stairs is to use a single 2 × 6 or a pair of 2 × 6s for each tread. Span is figured by multiplying the run by the number of treads. The span lets you locate the end of the stairway and position support posts.

Building stairs is often the most complicated part of any playground structure. To make the process as easy as possible, all of the calculations have already been made and the correct measurements are provided for each project. A detail of the stringers is also provided to help you build the stairs.

While each project in this section specifies how the stairs should be built, this page shows some variations in the event you'd like to try something else. You may want to incorporate a landing, which is really just an oversized step. It provides a convenient spot to change the direction of the stairway, and is a great place for children to catch their breath while climbing. Landings should be at least 36" square, or as wide as the staircase itself. They very often require reinforcement with diagonal cross braces between the support posts.

Open steps have metal cleats that hold the treads between the stringers. The treads on this stairway are built with two 2 × 6s to match the surface decking.

Boxed steps are built with notched stringers and solid risers to give a finished look to a deck stairway. Pre-drill the ends of treads to prevent splitting.

Long stairways sometimes require landings. A landing is a small platform to which both flights of stairs are attached.

Rails

Railings must be sturdy and firmly attached to the framing members of the play structure. Railing posts should never be attached to the surface of the decking. They should be fastened to the deck framing or deck fascia boards.

Most building codes require that railings be at least 36" above decking. Vertical balusters should be spaced fairly close together as a safety precaution.

To give your play structure railing a customized look, you can install pre-fabricated railing inserts, which come in a variety of designs. You can also paint the railing to match or complement the play structure. Painted railings create an elegant contrast to the natural wood colors found in the decking boards and stair treads.

The play structure plans in this section detail particular railing and baluster designs. Several are also featured below in case you would like to substitute alternative designs.

Vertical balusters with posts and rails are a popular choice for children's structures.

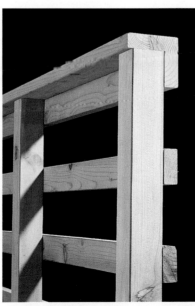

Horizontal railings are made of vertical posts, two or more wide horizontal rails, and a railing cap.

Lattice panels add a decorative touch to play structures. They also provide extra privacy.

Tools & Materials

6-ft. steel fence post
36¾" tubular steel ladder rungs (10)
4", 5", 6½", 7", 7½", 11"
carriage bolts with washers
⁵⁄₁₆ × 1½", ⁵⁄₁₆ × 2½", ⁵⁄₁₆ × 3½"
galvanized lag screws with washers
⅜ × 1½", ⅜ × 4", ⅜ × 5½",
2", 2½", 3" galvanized deck screws
Angled metal braces (4)
16" 2 × 2 treated stakes (6)
Metal A-frame gusset and brace plates
Swing hanger clamps (6)
#10 × 1½" sheet metal screws
String
¾" galvanized hex bolts with lock washers
Angle irons with ¾" screws (2)
4" mending plates with
¾" screws (2)

Swing & Slide with Tower

The play structure shown here has been carefully designed to provide fun and safe activity areas for your children. The ladders leading up to the clubhouse tower are angled to maximize the play areas above and below the structure.

Balusters and stringers frame all entrances and exits to enclose the deck, reducing the risk of injuries due to falls. In addition, milled cedar timbers are used in the construction to soften sharp corners and prevent splintering.

These directions are for building the basic tower with attached swing beam. A variety of accessories can easily be added to keep children challenged and entertained for years to come. Page 43 shows other options that are available.

The structure is anchored into the ground with wooden stakes to prevent any movement and to ensure safety for your kids as they play.

EXPLODED VIEW

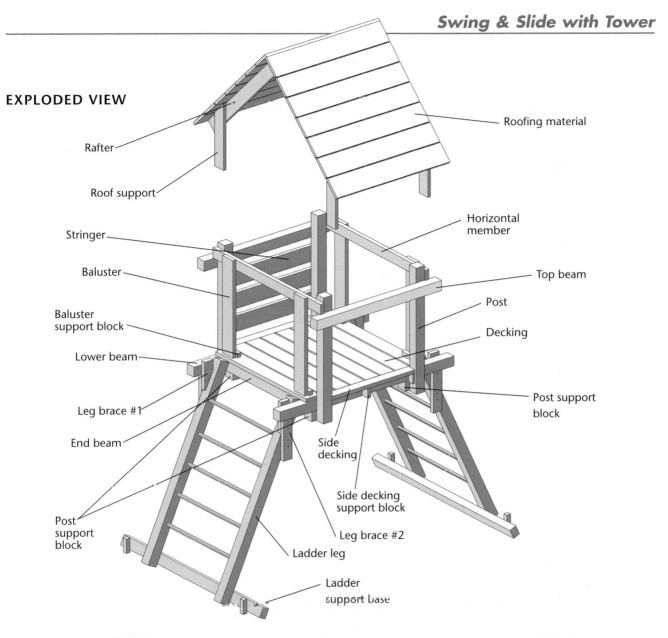

Rafter

Roof support

Stringer

Baluster

Baluster
support block

Lower beam

Leg brace #1

End beam

Post
support
block

Roofing material

Horizontal
member

Top beam

Post

Decking

Post support
block

Side
decking

Side decking
support block

Leg brace #2

Ladder leg

Ladder
support base

LUMBER LIST

PART	QTY.	SIZE	PART	QTY.	SIZE
Ladder leg	4	4 × 4 × 70"	Side decking support block	4	1 × 4 × 2¼"
Ladder support base*	2	3 × 4 × 72"	Side decking mid-support block (not shown)	2	2 × 4 × 3½"
Lower beam	2	4 × 4 × 71"	Stringer	3	¾ × 6 × 37"
Leg brace #1	4	2 × 4 × 12¾"	Baluster	4	¾ × 6 × 34"
Leg brace #2	4	2 × 4 × 15¼"	Baluster support block	4	2 × 2 × 7"
Decking	8	¾ × 6 × 47"	Rafter**	4	2 × 4 × 39"
Deck end beam, mid-beam (not shown)	3	4 × 4 × 41"	Roofing material***	14	1 × 6 × 66"
Post	4	4 × 4 × 44"	Double swing beam	2	4 × 4 × 113"
Post support block	4	4 × 4 × 7"	A-frame leg	2	4 × 4 × 96"
Top beam	2	4 × 4 × 51"	A-frame brace	1	2 × 4 × 41"
Horizontal member	2	2 × 4 × 56"	A-frame support base*	1	3 × 4 × 96"
Roof support **	4	2 × 4 × 18"			
Side decking	2	1 × 4 × 34"			

Use cedar building materials unless otherwise noted

*Landscape timber stock

**Treated lumber

***Tongue-and-groove cedar

Note: When working with treated lumber, hot-dipped galvanized
or stainless steel nails, fasteners, and fittings are recommended.

HOW TO BUILD THE TOWER & SWING BEAM

Step A: Assemble the Ladders

1. Cut four 4 × 4 ladder legs at 70" using a reciprocating saw. Draw a reference line down the middle of each leg using a straightedge. Measuring from one end, mark each leg along the reference line at 3¾", 13", 24", 35", 46", and 57".

2. At the 3¾" mark, drill a ⅜" hole through each ladder leg. At the remaining marks, drill 1⅜" deep holes using a 1⁵⁄₁₆" Forstner bit or spade bit, then round over the edges of each hole to a ¼" radius using a round file.

3. Drive five 36¾" tubular steel ladder rungs into the holes of one ladder leg using a scrap 2 × 4 and a mallet. Check the alignment of the rungs with a framing square to make sure they are perpendicular to the ladder legs. If the rungs are difficult to insert, apply petroleum jelly to the inside of the holes. **Note:** Loose rungs can be tightened by inserting aluminum flashing into the holes. Cut the flashing into ¾ × 2" strips, then install so the edges are ⅛" inside the edges of the holes.

4. Align the rungs with the holes in the second ladder leg and fit them in place. Place a scrap 2 × 4 over the leg and use a mallet to drive the rungs into the holes of the second leg, creating a 41" wide ladder. Repeat steps 2 through 4 to build the second ladder.

Step B: Build the Clubhouse Leg Assembly

1. Cut two 4 × 4 lower beams at 71". Measure from each end and make a mark at 8¾", centered on the beams. Drill ⅜" holes through the lower beams at each mark, then drill ⅝" deep counterbored holes using a 1⅜" spade bit.

2. On the side of the beams opposite the counterbored holes, measure from each end along the top edge and make a mark at 7⅝". Measure along the bottom edge and make a mark at 6". Connect the two marks using a straightedge and draw a reference line so the washers and nuts fit in the counterbored holes.

3. Place the ladders between the lower beams with the counterbored holes facing out. Align the counterbored holes with the holes at the top of the ladder legs. Use a ratchet wrench to loosely fasten the structure together using 7" galvanized carriage bolts with washers. See Lower Beam Detail, below.

Step C: Assemble the Leg Braces

1. Cut four 2 × 4 leg brace #1s at 12¾" and four leg brace #2s at 15¼" using a circular saw. On one end of each leg brace #1, measure 4¼" from the corner along the top edge and make a mark. Measure 2" down from the same corner along the outside edge and make a mark. Connect the two marks using a straightedge, then cut along the line.

2. Align the ladder legs with the reference lines drawn on the beams, then clamp leg brace #1 in

A. *Insert the rungs into one ladder leg using a mallet and scrap board. Lift the assembly and fit the rungs into the holes of the second leg.*

B. *Position the two ladders between the lower beams, align the pilot holes, and loosely fasten with carriage bolts.*

LOWER BEAM DETAIL

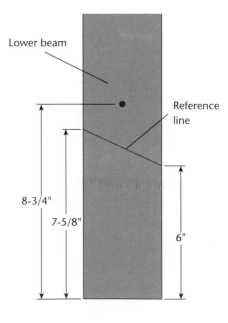

Lower beam

Reference line

8-3/4"

7-5/8"

6"

place so the angled edge rests on the ladder leg and the top is 1¼" above the top face of the lower beam.

3. From the top of leg brace #1, measure down and make a mark at 2" and 4" on-center. Drill 5⁄16" pilot holes through the braces at each location, then drill ¼" deep counterbored holes using a 1⅛" spade bit. Insert 5⁄16 × 2½" galvanized lag screws with washers through brace #1 and into the lower beam.

4. Clamp leg brace #2 to leg brace #1 so the outside edges are flush and leg brace #2 is butted against the outside face of the beam. From the top of leg brace #2, measure down and make a mark at 2", 4¼", 11", and 13¼", centered on the brace.

5. Drill 5⁄16" pilot holes through the braces at each mark, then drill ¼" deep counterbored holes in the pilot holes using a 1⅛" spade bit. Fasten leg brace #2 in place using 5⁄16 × 2½" galvanized lag screws with washers.

6. Brace the next corner the same way, then raise and brace the other side of the structure. Fully tighten the carriage bolts joining the lower beams to the ladder legs.

Step D: Install the End Beams & Mid-Beam

1. Cut eight 5⁄4 × 6 decking boards to 47" using a circular saw. Place one decking board across the lower beams at each end, tight against the tops of the ladders, aligning the ends with the outside edge of the beams. Drill a pair of 3⁄32" pilot holes and use 2½" galvanized deck screws to fasten only one end of the decking boards to the lower beams.

2. Cut two 4 × 4 end beams at 41". Clamp the end beams to the underside of the decking boards, between the lower beams, and tight against the ladder legs.

3. Drill pairs of ¼" pilot holes through the lower beams and into the ends of the end beams, then drill ⅝" deep counterbored holes using a 1⅜" spade bit. Also drill ⅜" clearance holes 1" deep for lag screw shanks. Fasten the beams using ⅜ × 1½" galvanized lag screws with washers. Use a ratchet wrench and tighten until the unattached ends of the decking boards are flush with the outside edge of the lower beam.

4. Drill two 3⁄32" pilot holes through the unattached ends of the decking boards and fasten to the lower beam using 2½" galvanized deck screws.

5. Cut one 4 × 4 mid-beam at 41". Center it between the end beams and clamp it to the decking boards. Drill two ¼" pilot holes through the end beams into the mid-beam, then drill ½" deep counterbored holes using a 1⅜" spade bit. Drill ⅜" clearance holes, 1" deep, for the lag screw shanks. Fasten using ⅜ × 5½" galvanized lag screws with washers.

6. Fasten the decking boards to the mid-beam by drilling 3⁄32" pilot holes and using 2½" galvanized deck screws.

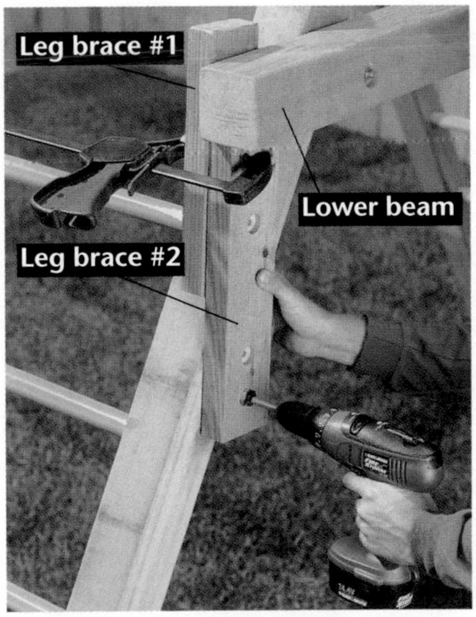

C. *Clamp the leg braces in place, drill counterbored pilot holes, and fasten to the ladder using lag screws with washers.*

LEG BRACE ASSEMBLY DETAIL

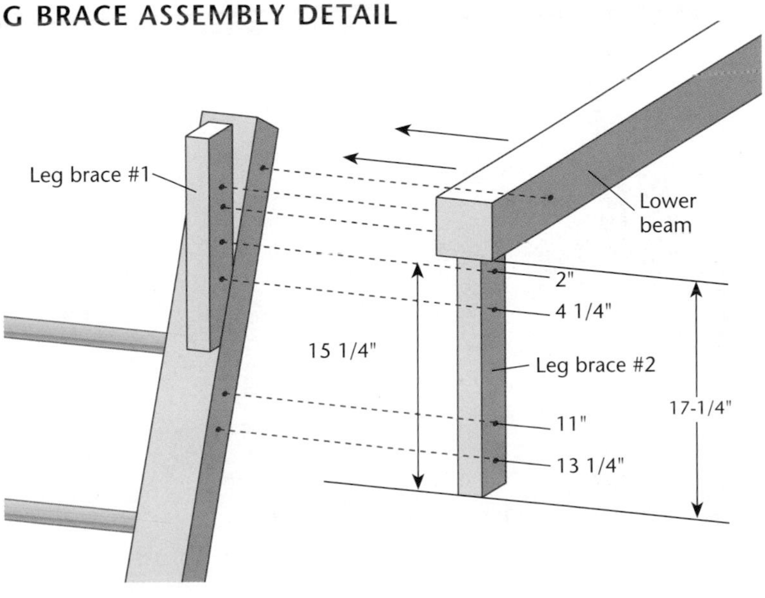

Step E: Add the Ladder Support Base

1. Cut two 3 × 4 landscape timbers at 72" for the ladder support bases, using a reciprocating saw.

2. Check to make sure the tower is level. Center the ladder support bases against the inside faces of the ladder legs. Set each base into the ground using a mallet.

3. Clamp the support bases to the ladders. Drill a ¼" pilot hole through each leg and into the base, then drill a ½"-deep counterbored hole using a 1⅜" spade bit. Drill ⅜" shank clearance holes 1" deep at each counterbored hole. Fasten the support bases using ⅜ × 5½" galvanized lag screws with washers.

4. To add strength and stability, attach angled metal braces between the ladders and the bases using 5⁄16 × 1½" galvanized lag screws. Drive 16"-long 2 × 2 pressure-treated stakes into the ground at each end of the bases. Attach the stakes to the support bases using 5⁄16 × 3½" galvanized lag screws.

Step F: Install the Decking & Posts

1. Evenly space the six remaining decking boards across the lower beams and mid-beam. Drill two 3⁄32" pilot holes in the decking over each beam, then fasten using 2½" galvanized deck screws.

2. Cut four 4 × 4 blocks at 7" to make post support blocks. Measure along one side of each block and mark the midpoint.

3. Measure from one end along each lower beam and make a mark at 16¾" and 54¼". Clamp the blocks to the underside of the lower beams, aligning the midpoint with each mark on the beams.

4. Drill a ¼" pilot hole through the bottom of each block into the lower beam, then drill 1¼" deep counterbored holes using a 1⅜" spade bit. Drill 1" deep, ⅜" shank clearance holes. Fasten the blocks using ⅜ × 4" lag screws with washers.

5. Cut four 4 × 4 posts at 44". Center the posts against the lower beams and blocks at the midpoint and align with the bottom edge of the blocks. Square the posts to the platform using a combination square, and clamp in place.

6. At each post, drill two ¼" pilot holes, one through the post and into the lower beam and one into the block. Drill ⅝"-deep counterbored holes using a 1⅜" spade bit. Drill ⅜" shank clearance holes to a 1" depth. Fasten the posts to the lower beams using 7" galvanized carriage bolts with washers and fasten to the blocks using ⅜ × 5½" galvanized lag screws with washers.

Step G: Install Top Beams & Horizontal Members

1. On the front side of the posts, measure down from the top and make a mark at 6".

2. Cut two 4 × 4 top beams at 51". Position the top beams across two posts, parallel to the lower beams, with the top edge of the top beams at the reference marks. Make sure the ends evenly overhang

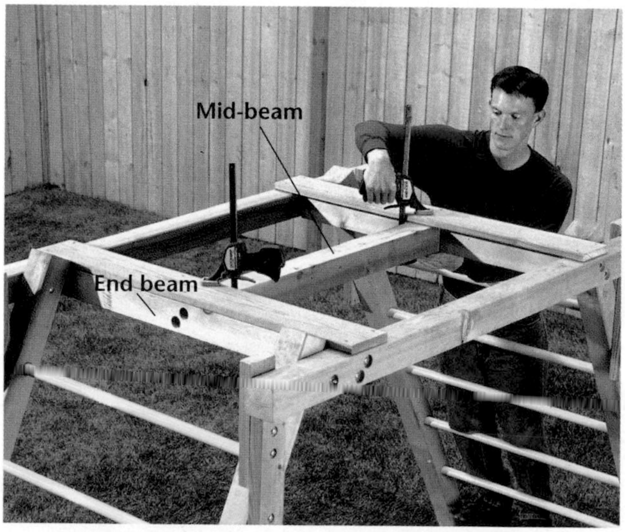

D. *Attach decking boards on top of the lower beams, set tightly against each ladder. Fasten on one side only. Position and secure the end beams and mid-beam, then fasten the other ends of the decking boards.*

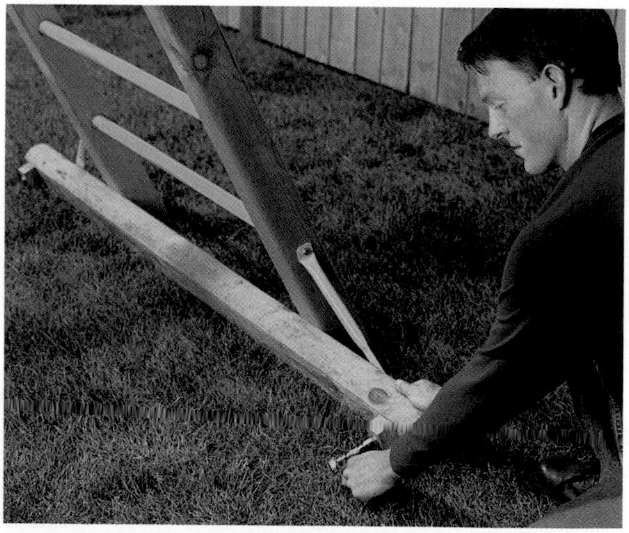

E. *Drive anchor stakes into the ground at each end of the base, then attach the stakes to the bases using lag screws.*

the sides of the posts, check for level, and clamp the beams in place.

3. Drill a ¼" pilot hole through each end of the top beams and into the posts, then drill ⅝" deep counter-bored holes using a 1⅜" spade bit. Drill ⅜" shank clearance holes to a 1" depth. Fasten the top beams to the posts using 7" galvanized carriage bolts with washers.

4. Cut two 2 × 4 horizontal members at 56". Cut four 2 × 4 roof supports at 18" and miter cut one end at a 45°.

5. On the ladder sides of the posts, measure down 1½" from the top and make a mark. Place the horizontal members across the posts, aligning the top edge with the marks and sandwiching the roof supports between the members and posts. Make sure the members are level, then clamp in place so the ends evenly overhang the posts. See Roof Support & Rafter Detail.

6. On the deck side of the posts, drill ⅜" pilot holes through the posts and roof supports into the horizontal members. Drill ½" deep counterbored holes using a 1⅜" spade bit and drill ⅜" shank clearance holes to a 1" depth. Fasten in place using 6½" galvanized carriage bolts with washers.

Step H: Install the Side Decking

1. Cut two 2 × 2 side decking support blocks at 2¼". On the swing side of the tower, place a block against each post so it is flush with the top of the lower beam. Drill two ³⁄₃₂" pilot holes, then fasten each block using 2" galvanized deck screws.

2. Cut one 1 × 4 side decking board at 34". Place the board on the blocks, drill a ³⁄₃₂" pilot hole at each end, then fasten using 2" galvanized deck screws.

3. Cut a 2 × 4 side decking mid-support block at 3½". Center the block against the lower beam so the top is flush with the underside of the side decking board. Drill a ³⁄₃₂" pilot hole through the block and into the lower beam, then drill a 1½"-deep counter-bored hole using a ⅞" spade bit. Fasten it in place using a 3" galvanized deck screw.

4. Drill a ³⁄₃₂" pilot hole through the top of the side decking board into the block. Fasten using a 2" galvanized deck screw.

5. Repeat these steps to install the side decking on the opposite side of the tower.

Step I: Install the Stringers & Balusters

1. Cut three ¾ × 6 stringers at 37". On the side of the tower with the side decking, clamp the stringers to the posts, spaced 2½" apart. Rip a scrap board to use as a spacer.

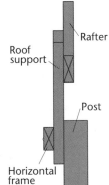

ROOF SUPPORT & RAFTER DETAIL

F. *Clamp the posts in place, making sure they are properly aligned and plumb (inset), then attach to the lower beams and support blocks using lag screws.*

G. *Attach the top beams to the posts, then attach the horizontal members and roof supports.*

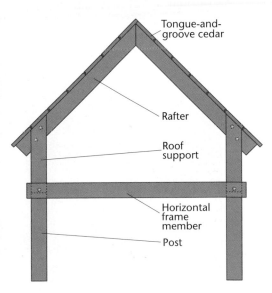

2. Drill two ³⁄₃₂" pilot holes through each stringer into the posts. Fasten the stringers using 2" galvanized deck screws.

3. Cut four ⁵⁄₄ × 6 balusters at 34". Cut four 2 × 2 baluster support blocks at 7". At one end of each baluster, fasten a block to the interior face, flush with the bottom edge. Drill two ³⁄₃₂" pilot holes, then fasten using 2" galvanized deck screws.

4. Position the balusters so they do not obstruct the ladder entrances to the tower, with the block ends on the deck and the tops against the horizontal members. Loosely fasten the top ends using 2" galvanized deck screws.

5. Check the balusters for plumb using a level, then drill a ³⁄₃₂" pilot hole through the blocks into the decking. Fasten the balusters using 2½" galvanized deck screws, then fully tighten the screws at the top end.

Step J: Build the Swing A-frame & Beam

1. On the swing side of the tower, install two angled metal braces extending from the lower beam to the posts using ⁵⁄₁₆ × 1½" galvanized lag screws.

2. Cut two 4 × 4 A-frame legs at 96" and one 2 × 4 A-frame brace at 41".

3. Place the legs on a flat surface. Measure from the top of the legs and make a mark at 1¾" and 44¾". At the 1¾" mark, drill ⅜" through holes centered on the legs. At the 44¾" mark, drill ⅜" through holes, then drill ½"-deep counterbored holes using a 1⅛" spade bit. Drill ⅜" through holes in each end of the brace, 1¾" from each end.

4. Attach the metal gusset to the inside face of the legs so the gusset flange faces up. Align the top screw holes of the gusset with the 1¾" through holes on the end of the legs. Attach the gusset using 4" galvanized carriage bolts so the washers and nuts are at the inside face. Loosely tighten each nut.

5. Position the brace against the outside face of the legs, aligning the through holes of the brace with the through holes at 44¾" on the legs. Fasten the brace to the legs using 5" galvanized carriage bolts so the washers and nuts fit in the counterbored hole. Loosely tighten each nut.

6. Adjust the A-frame legs to create a symmetrical triangle, then tighten all the nuts using a ratchet wrench. Drill a ⁷⁄₃₂" pilot hole in each leg at the remaining screw holes in the gusset, then secure using ⅜ × 1½" galvanized lag screws with washers.

7. Cut two 4 × 4 swing beams at 113". Clamp the beams together, then measure and make marks at 5¼", 19¾", 26⅞", 34", 49⅜", 56½", 63⅝", 79", 86⅛", 93¼", and 107¾".

8. Drill ⅜" holes through the beams at the marks. Drill 1½"-deep counterbored holes using a 1⅛" spade bit at the holes for 19¾", 34", 49⅜", 63⅝", 79", and

H. *Align a support block with the bottom of the side decking and attach it to the lower beam. Attach the side decking to the block.*

I. *Install stringers between the posts in the tower over any opening that does not house accessories.*

J. *Adjust the A-frame legs to form a symmetrical triangle, then fully tighten all the carriage bolts and install lag screws.*

93¼". Drill ¼" weep holes from the bottom edge of each counterbored hole out to the outer face of the beam for water drainage.

9. At the three pilot holes between the counterbored holes, use 7½" galvanized carriage bolts with washers to fasten the beams together.

10. Turn the beam so the bottom faces up. Install swing hanger clamps at the six counterbored pilot holes. Align each hanger clamp and fasten to the bottom beam with #10 × 1½" sheet metal screws. Secure the hangers at the top beam using washers and nuts.

Step K: Install the Swing A-frame & Beam

1. On the swing beam side of the clubhouse, run a level string between the two ladders at the bottom of their outside legs. Measure along the string from one end and mark the midpoint with masking tape.

2. Place the double swing beam on the ground, perpendicular to and 3½" out from the midpoint of the string. Check that the beam is square with the string using a framing square.

3. Drive a fence stake in the ground 1½" away from the far end of the beam. Position the A-frame in front

of the stake so it is perpendicular to and centered on the swing beam using a framing square. Secure the A-frame to the stake using string.

4. With a helper, lift the beam into place with one end on the gusset and the other end on the top beam of the tower.

5. Check that the swing beam is square and level, then align the hole in the end of the beam with the screw hole on the top of the gusset and fasten using a 7½" galvanized carriage bolt and washer.

6. At the tower, make sure the beam is centered on and square to the top beam. Using the pilot hole in the beam as a guide, drill a ⅜" pilot hole through the top beam. Fasten it in place using an 11" galvanized carriage bolt with washer.

7. Position angled metal braces to connect the swing beam and top beam. Drill ⁷⁄₃₂" pilot

SWING HANGER CLAMP DETAIL

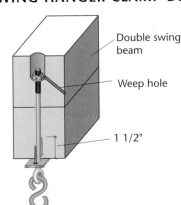

Double swing beam

Weep hole

1 1/2"

SWING A-FRAME & BEAM DETAIL

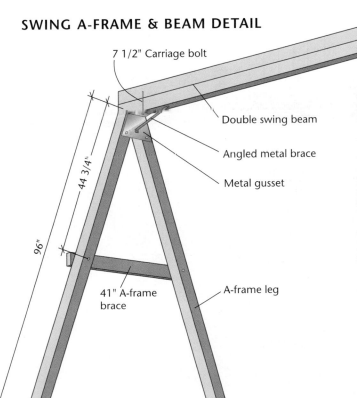

7 1/2" Carriage bolt

Double swing beam

Angled metal brace

Metal gusset

44 3/4"

96"

41" A-frame brace

A-frame leg

Brace plate

K. *With someone's help, lift the double swing beam into position. Make sure it is level and square, then fasten it to the gusset and the tower.*

holes, then fasten using ⅜ × 1½" galvanized lag screws with washers.

8. Drill a ⁷⁄₃₂" pilot hole in the bottom swing beam at the second screw hole of the gusset, then fasten using a ⅜ × 1½" galvanized lag screw. Attach an angled metal brace to the gusset and beam using a ¾" hex bolt, lock washer, and nut at the gusset. Drill a ⁷⁄₃₂" pilot hole at the beam location and insert a ⅜ × 1½" galvanized lag screw.

9. Connect the beam to the A-frame leg assembly using brace plates. Drill ⁷⁄₃₂" pilot holes, then fasten the plates using ⅜ × 1½" galvanized lag screws.

10. With the beam and A-frame in place, check to make sure the beam is level and the A-frame is plumb. Cut a 3 × 4 landscape timber leg support base at 96". Install the support base at the bottom of the leg assembly following the same techniques as in step E.

Step L: Build the Rafters

1. Cut four 2 × 4 rafters at 39" with a 45° angle on one end. Butt the angled ends of two rafters together. Install an angle iron at the bottom edge of the joint and fasten it using ¾" screws. Center a 4" mending plate over the joint and fasten it using ¾" screws.

2. Butt the rafter assemblies against the inside face of the roof supports with the mending plate facing into the structure and the top edge of the rafters aligned with the top of the roof supports. Clamp the rafters in place.

3. Drill two ³⁄₃₂" pilot holes in the rafters at the support locations. Fasten the rafters to the roof supports using 2½" galvanized deck screws.

Step M: Install the Roofing

1. Cut fourteen 1 × 6 tongue-and-groove cedar boards at 66". Position one board on top of the rafters, flush with the ends, with the tongue pointing toward the peak. Allow the ends to overhang the outside edges of the rafters by 6" on both sides, then clamp in place. Drill two ³⁄₃₂" pilot holes at both ends of the board, then fasten it to the rafters using 2" galvanized deck screws.

3. Working toward the peak, position subsequent boards so the groove fits over the tongue of the previous board. Overhang the rafters by 6" on each end. Drills pairs of ³⁄₃₂" pilot holes, then insert 2" galvanized deck screws.

4. If the last board overhangs the peak, position the board and mark the backside at the peak. Rip to size. Apply the roofing to the other side the same way.

L. *Butt the angled ends of the rafters together and secure the joint using an angle iron and a mending plate (inset). Align the rafter assembly with the roof supports and attach using deck screws.*

M. *Use tongue-and-groove cedar to cover the roof, fastening it to the rafters using deck screws. Allow the ends to overhang the rafters by 6".*

VARIATION: PLAY ACCESSORIES

A play structure is most fun when it provides a range of options. There is a wide variety of play equipment available, from simple favorites such as swings and slides to more elaborate equipment, like gliders, horizontal ladders, cargo nets, and rock climbing walls.

Other accessory items are designed to make play areas safer. Handles and railings help direct appropriate play routes, while shade walls and enclosures provide shaded areas for less active play. Most equipment and accessories are made of plastics or use powder-coat paints to provide non-slip, grippable surfaces.

Many of these items can be purchased at home centers or ordered directly from the manufacturer. Always follow the manufacturer's installation instructions when installing play structure accessories.

*A **sturdy slide** is a play structure standard, providing a thrilling ride out of the tower.*

*A **shade wall** shades the play area and provides a colorful alternative to wooden balusters or rails.*

*A **glider** is built to seat two, allowing children to swing together.*

*A **climbing wall** is a fun addition that creates a greater climbing challenge than a ladder.*

Backyard Playhouse

This 7½ × 8' playhouse has many of the architectural details you'd find on a real house, making it a truly special place to play—and a fun project to build. With two homemade windows and a door-window, the 5 × 8' interior of the main house is a bright, yet private, space. Outside, a 2½'-deep covered porch provides additional shelter for playing, lounging, or welcoming guests. The entire building is supported by a single floor frame attached to a wooden skid foundation, which helps make the playhouse easy to move.

As shown here, the simple design of the playhouse leaves plenty of room for you and your children to do your own decorating. The plan suggests the option of finishing the house interior with ¼" prefinished plywood paneling. You can also finish the ceiling by installing a few extra collar ties between the rafters and paneling over the roof frame.

For decorations and hardware, look through home accessory and hardware catalogs—they're full of decorative curiosities and interesting replica pieces perfect for adding charm to this little house.

MATERIALS LIST

DESCRIPTION	QTY./SIZE	MATERIAL
Foundation		
Drainage material	1 cu. yd.	Compactible gravel
Skids	3 @ 8'-0"	4 × 4 treated timbers
Floor Framing		
Rim joists	2 @ 8'-0"	2 × 6 treated
Joists	7 @ 8'-0"	2 × 6 treated
Joist clip angles	14 3" × 3" × 3" × 16-gauge galvanized	
Floor sheathing	2 sheets @ 4 × 8'	¾" tongue-and-groove, exterior-grade plywood
Decking	6 @ 9'-0"	1 × 6 treated
Wall Framing		
Plates	4 @ 8'-0", 4 @ 6'-0"	2 × 4
Studs	32 @ 6'-0", 2 @ 8'-0"	2 × 4
Headers	3 @ 6'-0"	2 × 6
Header spacers	3 @ 3'-0"	½" plywood—5" wide
Misc. framing	4 @ 10'-0"	2 × 4
Sheathing	7 sheets @ 4 × 8'	½" ext.-grade plywood
Interior paneling (optional)	7 sheets @ 4 × 8'	¼" plywood paneling
Porch Framing		
Posts	2 @ 5'-0"	4 × 4 cedar
Beam	1 @ 10'-0"	4 × 6 cedar
Post bases	2, with nails	Simpson BC40
Post/beam caps	2, with nails	Simpson BC4
Roof Framing		
Rafters	16 @ 8'-0"	2 × 4
Metal anchors—rafters	23, with nails	Simpson H2.5
Rafter straps	8 @ 12"-long	Simpson LSTA
Ridge board	1 @ 10'-0"	2 × 6
Lookouts	1 @ 6'-0"	2 × 4
Collar ties	1 @ 8'-0"	2 × 4
Roofing		
Roof sheathing	4 sheets @ 4 × 8'	½" ext.-grade plywood
Shingles	100 sq. ft.	250# per square (min.)
15# building paper	100 sq. ft.	
Metal drip edge	4 @ 10'-0"	Galvanized metal
Roof vents (optional)	2	
Exterior Finishes		
Siding	248 linear ft	8" cedar lap siding (6" exposure)
Subfascia	2 @ 10'-0"	1 × 4 pine
Fascia	2 @ 10'-0", 3 @ 8'-0"	1 × 6 S4S cedar
Fascia trim	2 @ 10'-0", 3 @ 8'-0"	1 × 2 S4S cedar
Corner trim	8 @ 6'-0"	1 × 4 S4S cedar
Deck trim	1 @ 9'-0", 1 @ 6'-0"	1 × 6 S4S cedar
Flashing—right side window	3'-0"	Galvanized—18-gauge
Plywood soffits	2 sheets @ 4 × 8'	⅜" cedar or fir plywood
Soffit vents	4 @ 4 × 12"	Louver w/bug screen
Window		
Frame	4 @ 6'-0"	¾ × 4¼" (actual) S4S cedar
Stops	8 @ 6'-0"	1 × 2 S4S cedar
Trim	8 @ 6'-0"	1 × 3 S4S cedar
Glazing tape	40 linear ft.	

DESCRIPTION	QTY./SIZE	MATERIAL
Window (cont.)		
Glass	2 pieces—field measure	¼" clear, tempered
Window grid (muntins)	2 @ 6'-0"	1 × 1 S4S cedar
Door		
Frame	2 @ 5'-0", 1 @ 3'-0"	¾ × 4¼" (actual) S4S cedar
Stops	2 @ 5'-0", 1 @ 3'-0"	1 × 2 S4S cedar
Panel material	8 @ 8'-0"	1 × 6 T&G V-joint S4S cedar
Window trim	4 @ 8'-0"	1 × 3 S4S cedar
Trim	5 @ 5'-0"	1 × 3 S4S cedar
Glass	1 piece—field measure	¼" clear, tempered
Strap hinges	3	
Railings (Optional)		
Top rail	1 @ 6'-0"	2 × 4 S4S cedar
Nailers	1 @ 6'-0"	2 × 2 S4S cedar
Balusters	8 @ 3'-0"	2 × 2 S4S cedar
Fasteners		
16d galvanized common nails		3½ pounds
16d common nails		2 pounds
10d common nails		1 pound
8d galvanized box nails		1½ pounds
8d box nails		2½ pounds
8d galvanized casing nails		24 nails
8d galvanized finish nails		½ pound
6d box nails		2 pounds
6d galvanized finish nails		½ pound
5d siding nails		2 pounds
3d galvanized box nails		¼ pound
1½" joist hanger nails		60 nails
⅞" galvanized roofing nails		1 pound
2½" deck screws		36 screws
2" deck screws		120 screws
1¼" wood screws		60 screws
Construction adhesive		4 tubes
Silicone-latex caulk		2 tubes
Miscellaneous		
6-ft. steel fence post		1
36¾" tubular steel ladder rungs		10
4", 5", 6½", 7", 7½", 11" carriage bolts with washers		
⁵⁄₁₆ × 1½", ⁵⁄₁₆ × 2½", ⁵⁄₁₆ × 3½", ⅜ × 1½", ⅜ × 4", ⅜ × 5½", galv. lag screws with washers		
2", 2½", 3" galvanized deck screws		
Angled metal braces		4
16" 2 × 2 treated stakes		6
Metal A-frame gusset		
Swing hanger clamps		6
#10 × 1½" sheet metal screws		
¾" galv. hex bolts with lock washers		
Angle irons with ¾" screws		2
4" mending plates with ¾" screws		2

Note: When working with treated lumber, hot-dipped galvanized or stainless steel nails, fasteners, and fittings are recommended.

HOW TO BUILD THE PLAYHOUSE

Step A: Build the Foundation & Floor Frame

1. Excavate the building site and add a 4" layer of compactible gravel. Tamp the gravel thoroughly, making sure it is level.

2. Cut three 4 × 4 treated timber skids at 95". Arrange and level the skids on the gravel bed.

3. Cut two 2 × 6 rim joists at 95" and seven joists at 86½". Mark the joist layout onto the rim joists 16" on center. Assemble the frame using 16d galvanized common nails, making sure to check each joist for crowning and install it with the crowned edge up.

4. Set the floor frame on top of the skids and measure the diagonals to make sure it's square. Install joist clip angles at each joist along the two outer skids, using 1½" joist hanger nails, and toenail each joist to the center skid using 16d nails.

5. Cut two pieces of plywood floor sheathing at 59". Install the first piece so the groove edge is flush with an end joist and one end is flush with the rear rim joist. Rip the tongue side of the second piece to fit and install it flush to the rear rim joist and opposite end joist. Use 8d galvanized box nails driven every 6" along the edges and every 12" in the field.

6. Cut six 1 × 6 decking boards at 98". Position the first board along the front edge of the floor frame so it overhangs the rim joist and both end joists by 1½". Fasten the board using 2" deck screws.

7. Install four more deck boards, leaving a gap between them if desired.

Note: You'll install the sixth board after adding the wall sheathing in Step G.

Step B: Frame the Walls

1. Snap chalk lines on the floor for the wall plates 3½" from the edge of the sheathing.

2. Cut four side wall plates at 59" and four front and rear wall plates at 88". Mark the stud layouts on the plates following the Floor Plan.

3. Cut twenty-six studs at 59½". Cut six jack studs at 54" for the window and door frames. Cut four sills at 27½" and six cripple studs at 23½".

4. Build the headers using two 2 × 6s with ½" plywood in the middle: two at 30½" for the windows and one at 33" for the door.

5. Assemble and raise the walls, setting them at the chalk lines. Brace the walls one at a time, then add the double top plates.

Step C: Install the Porch Posts & Beam

1. Cut two 4 × 4 posts at 48¼". Position the posts at the front corners of the porch 1½" in from the front edge and ends of the decking. Secure each post to the floor decking and frame with a metal post base using 16d galvanized nails. Plumb the posts using a level and install temporary cross braces to keep them in place.

2. Install a post/beam cap on top of each post.

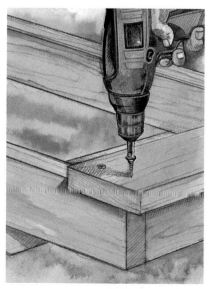

A. *Install the first deck board along the front edge of the floor frame, overhanging the front and sides by 1½".*

B. *Frame and raise the walls one at a time. Install the front wall flush with the edge of the plywood floor sheathing.*

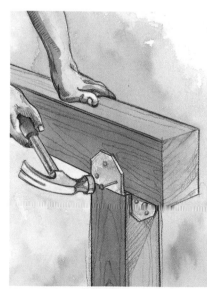

C. *Set the porch beam over the posts so it overhangs each end by 6" and secure the beam using nails.*

FRONT FRAMING ELEVATION

RIGHT SIDE FRAMING ELEVATION

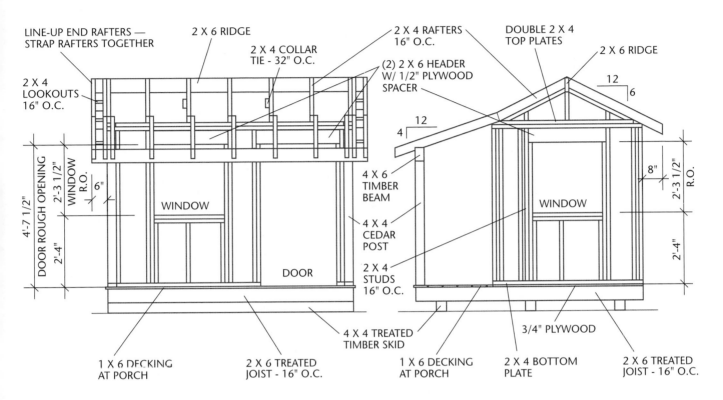

LINE-UP END RAFTERS —
STRAP RAFTERS TOGETHER

2 X 6 RIDGE

2 X 4 COLLAR
TIE - 32" O.C.

2 X 4
LOOKOUTS
16" O.C.

DOOR ROUGH OPENING
4'-7 1/2"

WINDOW
R.O.
2'-3 1/2"

6"

2'-4"

WINDOW

DOOR

1 X 6 DECKING
AT PORCH

2 X 6 TREATED
JOIST - 16" O.C.

2 X 4 RAFTERS
16" O.C.

DOUBLE 2 X 4
TOP PLATES

2 X 6 RIDGE

(2) 2 X 6 HEADER
W/ 1/2" PLYWOOD
SPACER

12
4

12
6

8"

2'-3 1/2"
R.O.

2'-4"

4 X 6
TIMBER
BEAM

4 X 4
CEDAR
POST

2 X 4
STUDS
16" O.C.

WINDOW

4 X 4 TREATED
TIMBER SKID

3/4" PLYWOOD

1 X 6 DECKING
AT PORCH

2 X 4 BOTTOM
PLATE

2 X 6 TREATED
JOIST - 16" O.C.

REAR FRAMING ELEVATION

LEFT SIDE FRAMING ELEVATION

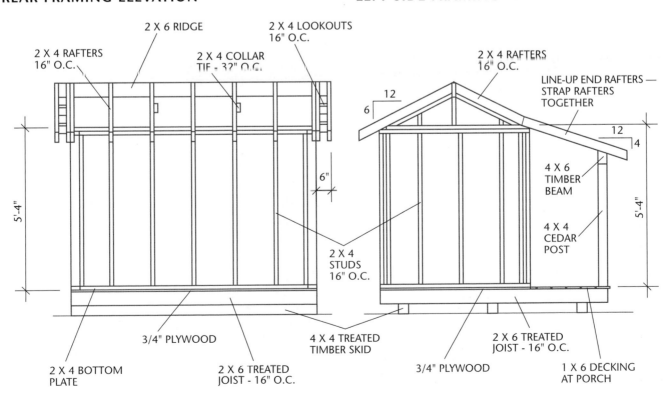

2 X 6 RIDGE

2 X 4 LOOKOUTS
16" O.C.

2 X 4 RAFTERS
16" O.C.

2 X 4 COLLAR
TIE - 32" O.C.

5'-4"

6"

2 X 4 RAFTERS
16" O.C.

LINE-UP END RAFTERS —
STRAP RAFTERS
TOGETHER

12
6

12
4

4 X 6
TIMBER
BEAM

4 X 4
CEDAR
POST

5'-4"

2 X 4
STUDS
16" O.C.

2 X 4 BOTTOM
PLATE

3/4" PLYWOOD

2 X 6 TREATED
JOIST - 16" O.C.

4 X 4 TREATED
TIMBER SKID

3/4" PLYWOOD

2 X 6 TREATED
JOIST - 16" O.C.

1 X 6 DECKING
AT PORCH

BUILDING SECTION

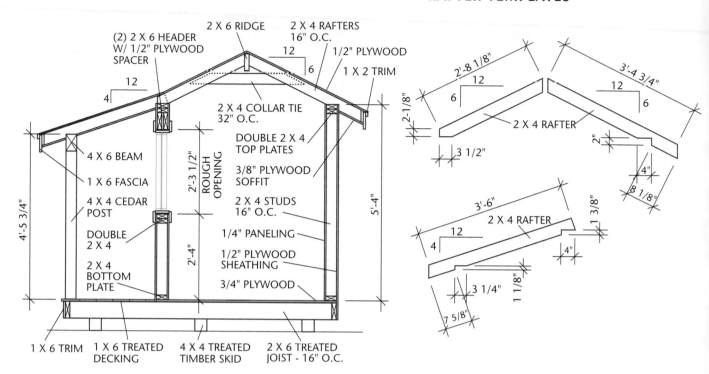

2 X 6 RIDGE

2 X 4 RAFTERS 16" O.C.

(2) 2 X 6 HEADER W/ 1/2" PLYWOOD SPACER

1/2" PLYWOOD

1 X 2 TRIM

12 / 4

12 / 6

2 X 4 COLLAR TIE 32" O.C.

DOUBLE 2 X 4 TOP PLATES

3/8" PLYWOOD SOFFIT

2 X 4 STUDS 16" O.C.

1/4" PANELING

1/2" PLYWOOD SHEATHING

3/4" PLYWOOD

4 X 6 BEAM

1 X 6 FASCIA

4 X 4 CEDAR POST

DOUBLE 2 X 4

2 X 4 BOTTOM PLATE

4'-5 3/4"

2'-3 1/2" ROUGH OPENING

2'-4"

5'-4"

1 X 6 TRIM

1 X 6 TREATED DECKING

4 X 4 TREATED TIMBER SKID

2 X 6 TREATED JOIST - 16" O.C.

RAFTER TEMPLATES

2'-8 1/8"

12 / 6

2-1/8"

3 1/2"

2 X 4 RAFTER

3'-4 3/4"

12 / 6

2"

4"

8 1/8"

3'-6"

12 / 4

2 X 4 RAFTER

1 3/8"

4"

3 1/4"

1 1/8"

7 5/8"

FLOOR FRAMING PLAN

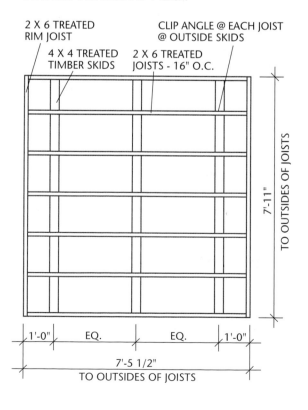

2 X 6 TREATED RIM JOIST

4 X 4 TREATED TIMBER SKIDS

CLIP ANGLE @ EACH JOIST @ OUTSIDE SKIDS

2 X 6 TREATED JOISTS - 16" O.C.

7'-11" TO OUTSIDES OF JOISTS

1'-0" EQ. EQ. 1'-0"

7'-5 1/2" TO OUTSIDES OF JOISTS

FLOOR PLAN

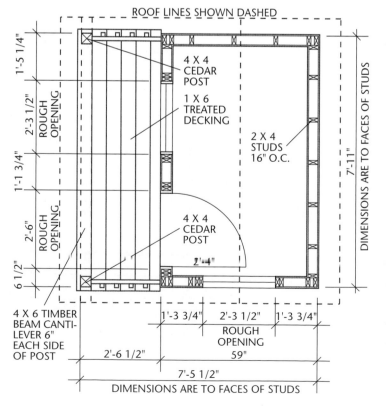

ROOF LINES SHOWN DASHED

4 X 4 CEDAR POST

1 X 6 TREATED DECKING

2 X 4 STUDS 16" O.C.

4 X 4 CEDAR POST

1'-5 1/4"

2'-3 1/2" ROUGH OPENING

1'-1 3/4"

2'-6" ROUGH OPENING

6 1/2"

2'-4"

7'-11" DIMENSIONS ARE TO FACES OF STUDS

4 X 6 TIMBER BEAM CANTI-LEVER 6" EACH SIDE OF POST

1'-3 3/4" 2'-3 1/2" 1'-3 3/4"

ROUGH OPENING

2'-6 1/2" 59"

7'-5 1/2"

DIMENSIONS ARE TO FACES OF STUDS

48

3. Cut the 4 × 6 beam at 107". Set the beam on top of the posts so it overhangs each end by 6". Measure diagonally between the posts to make sure the posts and beam are square, then fasten the beam to the post caps.

Step D: Frame the Roof

1. Cut two pattern rafters of each rafter type following the Rafter Templates. Test fit the rafters using a 2 × 6 spacer block. Cut the remaining common rafters so you have a total of seven of each type. For the gable overhang, cut four porch rafters without the upper bird's mouth; cut four rear house rafters (long ones) without bird's mouths; and cut four front house rafters without the level cut on the bottom end.

2. Cut the 2 × 6 ridge board at 107". Mark the rafter layout onto the wall plates and porch beam. Lay out the ridge board so the outsides of the outer common rafters are 6" from the ends.

3. Install the common rafters and ridge board. Secure the lower ends of the rafters to the wall plates and porch beam using metal anchors. Facenail the porch rafters to the house rafters using 10d nails.

4. Cut two 2 × 4 collar ties at 39", mitering the ends at about 26°. Position the ties against the rafter pairs that fall on either side of the center rafters, making sure they are level and their ends are ½" away from the top edges of the rafters. Facenail the ties to the rafters using three 10d common nails at each end.

5. Cut the gable wall plates to reach from the ridge to the wall plates. Install them with their outside edges flush with the outer rafters. Cut and install the gable studs.

Step E: Build the Gable Overhangs

1. Mark and cut the front and porch overhang rafters so they meet end-to-end. Clamp an overhang rafter against an outer house rafter. Set a porch overhang rafter in position so the end overhangs the clamped rafter using a straightedge to align it with the other porch rafters. Mark the two overhang rafters where they meet at the top and bottom edges. Draw a cutting line between the two marks, then make the cuts. Test fit the rafters, then use them as patterns to mark and cut three more pairs of overhang rafters.

2. Cut ten 2 × 4 lookouts at 3". Endnail the lookouts to each of the inner overhang rafters and porch rafters, using 16" on-center spacing with 16d nails.

3. Facenail the inner overhang rafters to the outer common rafters using 10d nails. Butt together the ends of the porch and front rafters and join them with metal straps and 8d nails.

4. Fasten the outer overhang rafters to the ridge and lookouts. Anchor the porch rafters using straps.

Step F: Install the Fascia, Sheathing & Roofing

1. Cut and install the 1 × 4 subfascia along the eaves using 8d box nails.

2. Install the 1 × 6 fascia and 1 × 2 fascia trim

D. *Install the rafters, adding anchors where they meet the front and rear house wall and the porch beam.*

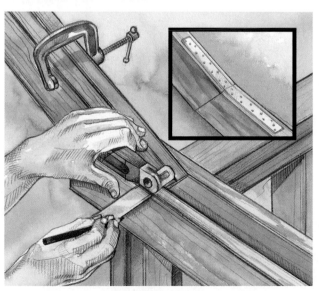

E. *Mark the gable overhang rafters for cutting so their ends can be butted together, then join them using metal straps (inset).*

FRONT ELEVATION

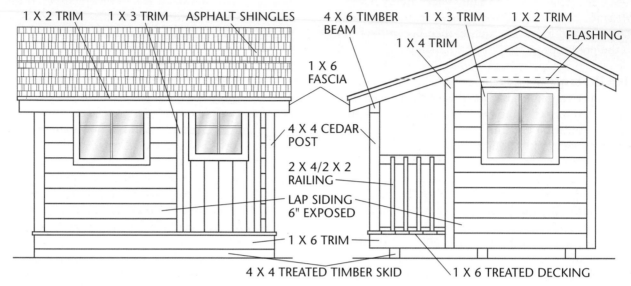

1 X 2 TRIM   1 X 3 TRIM   ASPHALT SHINGLES

LEFT SIDE ELEVATION

4 X 6 TIMBER BEAM   1 X 3 TRIM   1 X 2 TRIM

1 X 4 TRIM   FLASHING

1 X 6 FASCIA

4 X 4 CEDAR POST

2 X 4/2 X 2 RAILING

LAP SIDING 6" EXPOSED

1 X 6 TRIM

4 X 4 TREATED TIMBER SKID   1 X 6 TREATED DECKING

REAR ELEVATION

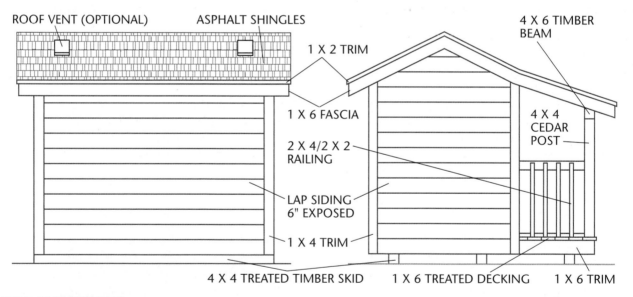

ROOF VENT (OPTIONAL)   ASPHALT SHINGLES

1 X 2 TRIM

1 X 6 FASCIA

2 X 4/2 X 2 RAILING

LAP SIDING 6" EXPOSED

1 X 4 TRIM

RIGHT SIDE ELEVATION

4 X 6 TIMBER BEAM

4 X 4 CEDAR POST

4 X 4 TREATED TIMBER SKID   1 X 6 TREATED DECKING   1 X 6 TRIM

DOOR ELEVATIONS

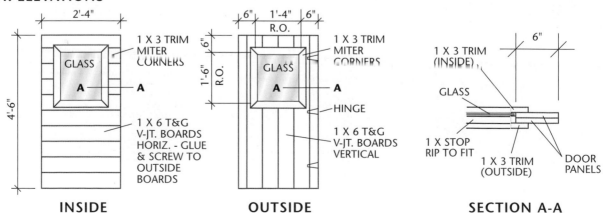

2'-4"

GLASS

A —————— A

4'-6"

1 X 3 TRIM MITER CORNERS

1 X 6 T&G V-JT. BOARDS HORIZ. - GLUE & SCREW TO OUTSIDE BOARDS

INSIDE

6"   1'-4"   6"
R.O.

6"

1'-6"
R.O.

GLASS

A —————— A

1 X 3 TRIM MITER CORNERS

HINGE

1 X 6 T&G V-JT. BOARDS VERTICAL

OUTSIDE

6"

1 X 3 TRIM (INSIDE)

GLASS

1 X STOP RIP TO FIT

1 X 3 TRIM (OUTSIDE)

DOOR PANELS

SECTION A-A

along the gable overhangs. Hold the fascia ½" above the rafters so it will be flush with the sheathing. Use 6d galvanized finish nails.

3. Install the fascia along the eaves, flush with the tops of the rafters, using a square or straightedge to align the fascia with the rafters. Install the 1 × 2 fascia trim so its top edge is flush with the top of the roof sheathing. Use a square and a scrap of ½" plywood to position the trim.

4. Install the ½" plywood sheathing, using 8d box nails. At the point where the house roof meets the porch roof, make sure the sheathing joints are aligned with the rafter joints.

5. Attach metal drip edge along the eaves and gable ends, then staple 15# building paper over the sheathing and drip edge.

6. Install the asphalt shingles, starting at the eave edge. If desired, install roof vents on the rear side of the roof.

Step G: Install the Wall Sheathing & Soffits

1. Install the ½" plywood wall sheathing to the framing using 6d box nails. Extend the sheathing from the bottom of the floor frame to the bottoms of the rafters and overlap the sheets at the wall corners.

2. Rip the final decking board to fit and install it.

3. Install the ⅜" plywood soffit panels, using 3d galvanized box nails. Bevel the soffit edges where they meet the fascia along the eaves, at the front of the porch, at the back side of the porch beam, and

wherever two panels meet.

4. Cut holes for four soffit vents. Locate one vent in each of the two outer rafter bays, along the rear eaves, and near the house under the porch roof. Install the soffit vents using screws.

Step H: Apply the Interior Finish, Build & Install the Windows

1. If desired, install ¼" prefinished plywood paneling over the framing using 1" finish nails. Cut the paneling flush with the rough openings.

2. Using ¾ × 4¼" stock, cut the window frame pieces to form two 27 × 27" frames (outer dimensions). Assemble the frame using 2" deck screws.

3. Install each frame in its rough opening using shims and 8d casing nails.

4. Cut sixteen 1 × 2 stops. Bevel the two outer sill stops. Attach the inner stops using 6d galvanized finish nails. Order the glass to fit.

5. Install the glass and outer stops, applying glazing tape to the stops on both sides of the glass.

6. Cut and install the 1 × 3 window trim. Make sure the outer trim pieces are plumb and level. To create the appearance of divided window panes, build window muntin bars from 1 × 1 cedar and attach them to the outer stops.

Step I: Build & Install the Door

1. Cut the head jamb for the door frame at 29⅝" and the two side jambs at 54¼". Position the head

F. *Use a square or straightedge set on a rafter to position the fascia.*

G. *Add soffit vents under the rear eaves and beneath the porch roof.*

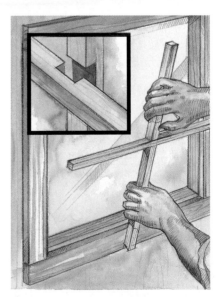

H. *Create muntins using two 1 × 1s joined with a half-lap joint.*

EAVES DETAIL (REAR)

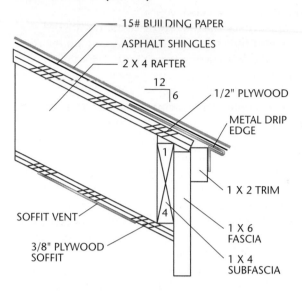

- 15# BUILDING PAPER
- ASPHALT SHINGLES
- 2 X 4 RAFTER
- 12
- 6
- 1/2" PLYWOOD
- METAL DRIP EDGE
- 1 X 2 TRIM
- 1 X 6 FASCIA
- 1 X 4 SUBFASCIA
- SOFFIT VENT
- 3/8" PLYWOOD SOFFIT

GABLE OVERHANG DETAIL

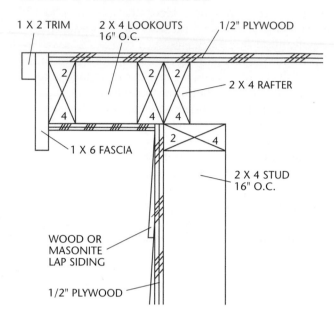

- 1 X 2 TRIM
- 2 X 4 LOOKOUTS 16" O.C.
- 1/2" PLYWOOD
- 2 X 4 RAFTER
- 1 X 6 FASCIA
- 2 X 4 STUD 16" O.C.
- WOOD OR MASONITE LAP SIDING
- 1/2" PLYWOOD

WINDOW JAMB DETAIL

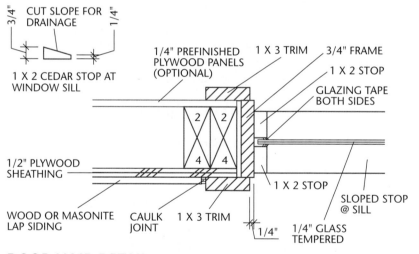

- 3/4"
- CUT SLOPE FOR DRAINAGE
- 1/4"
- 1 X 2 CEDAR STOP AT WINDOW SILL
- 1/4" PREFINISHED PLYWOOD PANELS (OPTIONAL)
- 1 X 3 TRIM
- 3/4" FRAME
- 1 X 2 STOP
- GLAZING TAPE BOTH SIDES
- 1/2" PLYWOOD SHEATHING
- 1 X 2 STOP
- WOOD OR MASONITE LAP SIDING
- CAULK JOINT
- 1 X 3 TRIM
- 1/4"
- 1/4" GLASS TEMPERED
- SLOPED STOP @ SILL

DOOR JAMB DETAIL

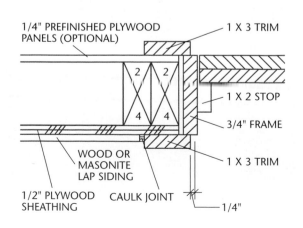

- 1/4" PREFINISHED PLYWOOD PANELS (OPTIONAL)
- 1 X 3 TRIM
- 1 X 2 STOP
- 3/4" FRAME
- 1 X 3 TRIM
- WOOD OR MASONITE LAP SIDING
- 1/2" PLYWOOD SHEATHING
- CAULK JOINT
- 1/4"

RAILING SECTION

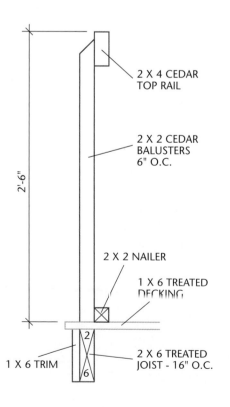

- 2 X 4 CEDAR TOP RAIL
- 2 X 2 CEDAR BALUSTERS 6" O.C.
- 2'-6"
- 2 X 2 NAILER
- 1 X 6 TREATED DECKING
- 1 X 6 TRIM
- 2 X 6 TREATED JOIST - 16" O.C.

jamb over the ends of the side jambs and fasten the pieces using 2" deck screws. Cut and install the 1 × 2 stops 1½" from the inside edges of the frame. If you want the door to swing out, install the stops 1½" from the outside edges.

2. Cut out the bottom plate from the door rough opening. Install the frame using shims and 8d casing nails, making sure the frame is square and plumb.

3. Cut six 1 × 6 tongue-and-groove boards at 54". Fit them together and trim the two outer boards so the total width is 28".

4. Cut eleven 1 × 6 tongue-and-groove boards at 28". Fit the boards together with their ends flush, then trim the outer boards so the total length is 54".

5. Mark the rough opening for the door window onto the outside face of the door. Glue the two sides of the door together using construction adhesive, then drive 1¼" screws through the back side. Cut out the window opening using a circular saw and handsaw.

6. Cut the 1 × 3 trim to fit around the window opening so it overlaps the opening by ¾". Attach the trim to the inside door face using 6d galvanized finish nails. Order the glass to fit.

7. Install the glass with glazing tape on both sides, then rip the 1 × 3 stops to fit between the glass and the outside door face. Install the stops using 6d finish nails, then cut and install the trim on the outside face. If desired, install 1 × 1 muntins (see Step H).

8. Mount the hinges and hang the door, then install the 1 × 3 trim on both sides of the door. Make sure the trim is plumb and level.

Step J: Install the Corner Trim & Siding

1. Install the 1 × 4 corner trim using 8d galvanized finish nails. Hold the trim ¾" below the bottom of the floor frame and overlap the trim at the corners. Install 1 × 6 trim along the porch portion of the floor frame.

2. Install flashing above the right-side window, then install the lap siding. Start the first courses flush with the trim ends and butt the siding ends against the trim.

3. Caulk all joints where the siding meets the trim.

Step K: Install the Railings (Optional)

1. Cut two 2 × 4 cedar top rails to fit between the corner trim and the porch posts. Install the rails so their outer faces are 1½" from the outsides of the posts and their top edges are 30" above the porch deck using 2½" deck screws.

2. Cut two 2 × 2 nailers to fit between the corner trim and posts, 1½" in from the outsides of the posts. Attach them to the decking using 2½" deck screws.

3. Cut eight 2 × 2 cedar balusters at 28½" with a 45° on one end. Fasten the balusters to the rails and nailers using deck screws, keeping an even spacing between the balusters.

I. Install stops against the glass with their edges flush with the door face.

J. Cut the lap siding to fit snugly between the trim boards.

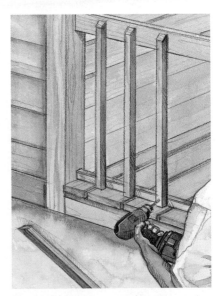

K. Attach the balusters to the railings and nailers using 2½" deck screws.

Log Fort with Bridge

This is the fort you wish you had when you were a kid. Its three-legged structure and bridge conjure up images of pirates, secret hideaways, and buried treasure. The fort is primarily constructed with 6" logs and rope to give it a rugged outdoor look.

It's only fair to warn you upfront that this fort is not easy to build. The logs are heavy, and all of the corners and rafters require angled cuts. The logs also need to be notched. With that said, we also want to assure you that it is certainly a project that can be built using these directions and some patience.

The logs for this project are not readily available at all lumberyards and home improvement centers, so you may have to special order them. You can substitute 6 × 6 square beams for the logs and adjust the cuts and notches as necessary. To make the project easier, you can ask a lumberyard or home improvement center to make the angled cuts in the lumber for you or recommend a place that will. On a final note, you'll notice the drawings do not include dimensions for the fascia and beams. You'll need to measure the distances yourself, and for good reason. The chances that all of your corner posts will be perfectly straight and plumb are minimal. If one post is off just a little bit, it will impact the measurements, especially at the top of the structure, so it's best to take the measurements yourself to ensure the boards are cut to the appropriate lengths.

MATERIAL LIST

DESCRIPTION	QTY./SIZE	MATERIAL
Support System		
Log post	4 @ 13'-0"	6"-diameter treated log
Floor Framing		
Log beams	3 @ 8'-0"	6"-diameter treated log
Joist, rim joists, blocking	6 @ 6'-0"	2 × 4 treated
Decking	13 @ 6'-0"	2 × 6 treated
Spikes	10 @ 7"	Rim joist to log
Spikes	12 @ 7"	Log to log
Roof Framing		
Rafters	9 @ 6'-0"	2 × 6
		SPF construction grade no.2
Hip rafters	6 @ 8'-0"	2 × 6
		SPF construction grade no.2
Beams	6 @ 8'-0"	2 × 8
		SPF construction grade no.2
Roofing sheathing	6 @ 4' × 8'	½" APA-rated plywood
Rafter hold down clips	15 with nails	Simpson H1
Hold down straps	3 with nails	Simpson ST12
Roof		
Shingles	54 square feet	Asphalt shingles
		minimum 250# per square
Roofing felt	54 square feet	15# roofing felt
Metal roof edge	3 @ 12'-0"	Galvanized metal
Galvanized roofing nails	⅞" – 1½ pounds	Shingles to roof sheathing
Exterior Finishes		
Fascia trim	3 @ 12'-0"	1 × 6 S4S cedar
Fort Railing		
Top and bottom rails	10 @ 8'-0"	2 × 6 S4S cedar
Rope railing	¾" @ 160'-0"	Nylon rope
Rope anchors	12 @ 4"	Lag eye bolt
Stair Railing		
Top and bottom rails	4 @ 8'-0"	2 × 6 S4S cedar

DESCRIPTION	QTY./SIZE	MATERIAL
Stair Railing (cont.)		
Rope railing	¾" @ 138'-0"	Nylon rope railing
Thru bolts w/washers	16 @ ⅜ × 8"	Rails to post
Rope anchors	8 @ 4"	Lag eye bolt
Bridge		
Rope railing	¾" @ 84'-0"	Nylon rope railing
Decking	20 @ 3'-6"	3 × 3 treated
Chain	2 @ 6'-0"	5⁄16"-thick chain
Chain connectors	4	Chain to eye bolt
Eye bolt with washers	8 @ ⅜ × 7"	Railing to post,
		bridge chain to post
Rope anchors	4 @ 4"	Lag eye bolt
Stairs		
Stringer	2 @ 8'-0"	2 × 12 treated
Risers	6 @ 3'-0"	2 × 12 treated
Top riser	1 @ 3"	2 × 8 treated
Riser supports	12	2" × 1½" × 8"
		12-gauge galvanized angle
Top riser supports	2	2" × 1½" × 6"
		12-gauge galvanized angle
Log post	2 @ 11'-0"	6"-diameter treated post
Log post	2 @ 7'-6"	6"-diameter treated post
Galvanized wood screws	1¼"	Riser supports
Thru bolts w/washers	6 @ ⅜ × 8"	Stringer to post
Miscellaneous		
Galvanized box nails	16d – 5 pounds	Lumber to lumber
Galvanized box nails	8d – 2 pounds	Roof beams to posts
Box nails	6d – 2 pounds	Sheathing to lumber
Galvanized finish nails	16d – 2 pounds	Rails
Galvanized finish nails	6d – 1 pound	Trim
Galvanized wood screws	80 @ 2½"	Decking to joists

Note: When working with treated lumber, hot-dipped galvanized or stainless steel nails, fasteners, and fittings are recommended.

HOW TO BUILD A LOG FORT WITH BRIDGE

Step A: Dig Holes for the Posts

1. Set up batter boards and run mason's line to form a 72 × 193⅜" rectangle. Keep the lines tight. Take diagonal measurements between corners to make sure the lines are square to each other.

2. Measure 36" from the right side corners and make a mark on pieces of tape attached to the front and rear lines. Set up another set of batter boards and run another mason's line so the line crosses the 36" marks. Measure the diagonal distance between

FLOOR PLAN

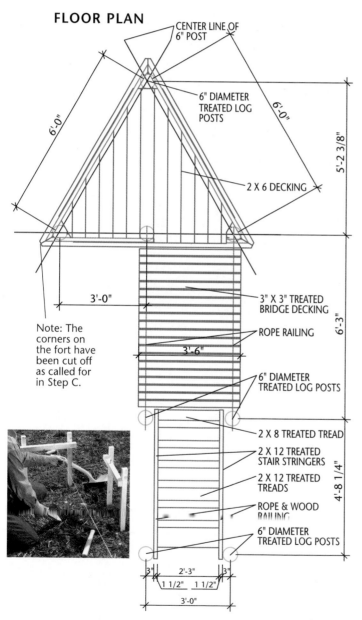

CENTER LINE OF 6" POST

6" DIAMETER TREATED LOG POSTS

6'-0"

6'-0"

5'-2 3/8"

2 X 6 DECKING

3'-0"

3" X 3" TREATED BRIDGE DECKING

ROPE RAILING

6'-3"

3'-6"

6" DIAMETER TREATED LOG POSTS

2 X 8 TREATED TREAD

2 X 12 TREATED STAIR STRINGERS

2 X 12 TREATED TREADS

ROPE & WOOD RAILING

6" DIAMETER TREATED LOG POSTS

4'-8 1/4"

3" 2'-3" 3"
1 1/2" 1 1/2"
3'-0"

Note: The corners on the fort have been cut off as called for in Step C.

A. *Set up batter boards and run mason's lines to mark the locations of the posts.*

corners to make sure they're square.

3. Measure 62⅜" from the back corners and mark pieces of tape attached to the right and left side mason's lines. Measure 56¼" from the front corners and mark pieces of tape attached to the right side and center mason's lines. Set up batter boards and run mason's lines to cross the 62⅜" and the 56¼" marks. Measure diagonally between corners to ensure the lines are square.

4. Find the centerpoint of each post location by hanging a plumb bob at the line intersections, then drive stakes into the ground at the marks. Remove the mason's lines and take down the batter boards. At the post locations, dig holes 48" deep for the four fort posts and 42" deep for the four stair posts using a power auger. If you're adding gravel, add 4" to the depth of the holes.

Step B: Set the Posts

1. Set the posts in the holes. Build temporary bracing by attaching a 2 × 4 to a post at a 45° angle. Drive a long 2 × 4 stake in the ground at the end of the brace. Plumb the post using a level, then fasten the brace to the stake. Attach a second brace to an adjacent side of the post so the post is perfectly plumb. Do this for each post. Keep in mind that the posts are very heavy and the braces must be securely staked to hold the posts in place.

Note: If you're setting the posts in clay soil, add 4" of compactible gravel to each hole before inserting the posts.

2. Backfill the holes with soil. Pack the soil around

B. *Wrap paper around each post at the mark, then draw along the edge of paper to give yourself a cutting line around the entire post.*

the posts.

3. On the front middle post of the fort, measure up from the ground and make marks at 48", 90", and 108". Use a long, straight board and a level to transfer the 48" measurement to the two posts for the front of the stairs, the 90" measurement to the two posts at the front of the bridge, and the 108" measurement to the other three posts for the fort.

4. Wrap a sheet of paper around a post, keeping the edge of the paper at the mark. Overlap the paper a few inches. Mark the post around the edge of the paper. Do this for each post, then cut the posts at the marks using a reciprocating saw or handsaw.

Step C: Attach the Log Beams

1. Measure 65" from the top of the fort posts and make a mark. Below each mark, cut a notch in the outside edges of the posts 1¼" deep × 6" long by making several horizontal cuts with a reciprocating saw. Knock out the notch using a hammer and chisel.

2. Cut three 6" diameter logs at 91" with a 30° angle on each end. Make the cuts using a large miter saw. You can also start the cuts with a miter saw and finish with a handsaw.

3. Set a log in the notches on one side of the fort so the ends of the log extend 9½" past the center of each post. Mark the log at the notch. Take the log down and cut a 1¼" deep notch at the marks. Set the log in place and make sure it's level. You may need to make additional cuts in the notches for a perfect fit. Drive two 7" spikes through the log into the post at each end.

4. Place a log in the notches on the next side so the end is flush with the first log. Mark and cut notches, then set it back in place. Make sure the log is level, then fasten it to the posts using spikes. Do the same for the third log so the ends are flush with the others.

5. The corners where the logs come together are sharp and pose a safety hazard. Cut 3" off the ends of the logs at the corners for a blunt edge.

Step D: Frame the Deck

1. Cut two 2 × 4 rim joists at 60¾" with a 60° angle on each end. Cut two rim joists at 27⅜" with a 30° angle on one end and square on the other end.

2. Measure 12⅛" from the end of each log where it's been cut off and make a mark on the top of the log. Place a 60¾" rim joist on-edge on the top center of the left and right side logs so the ends are at the 12⅛" marks. Place the 27⅜" joists on either side of the front middle posts, aligning the outside ends with the 12⅛" marks. Drill pilot holes and nail the rim joists to the logs using 7" spikes. The long rim joists get 3 spikes apiece, the short ones get a spike at each end.

3. Measure the distance between the ends of the rim joists installed in the last step and cut three joists to that measurement with a 60° angle on each end. Place these joists between the ends of the rim joists and nail them to the rim joists and posts using 16d box nails.

4. Measure from the back ends of the right and left side rim joists and make a mark for the joists 24" on-center. Measure the distance between each

C. *Cut notches in the posts (inset) and logs, then set the logs in the notches in the posts. Make sure the angled ends fit tightly together.*

RAILING DETAIL

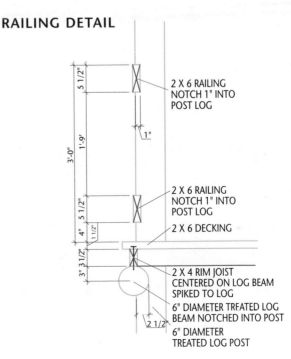

2 X 6 RAILING NOTCH 1" INTO POST LOG

2 X 6 RAILING NOTCH 1" INTO POST LOG

2 X 6 DECKING

2 X 4 RIM JOIST CENTERED ON LOG BEAM SPIKED TO LOG

6" DIAMETER TREATED LOG BEAM NOTCHED INTO POST

6" DIAMETER TREATED LOG POST

5 1/2"

3'-0"

1'-9"

5 1/2"

4"

1 1/2"

1"

3" 3 1/2"

2 1/2"

set of marks and cut 2 × 4 joists to those measurements with a 60° angle on each end. Set the joists at the marks and attach them by endnailing through the rim joists using 16d nails.

5. Measure the distance between the ends of the rim joists on the front side of the fort and the nearer center joist. Cut two blocks to that measurement and nail them to the ends of the rim joists. Use a framing square to square the blocks to the rim joists, then nail them to the face of the middle joist using 16d nails. Cut a block at 6" and nail it to the inside face

of the middle post between the two longer blocks; also nail the ends to the longer blocks.

Step E: Install the Deck Boards

1. Cut a 2 × 6 deck board at 56⅜" and center it on the rim joists between the back post and front center post. Drill two ³⁄₃₂" pilot holes in each end of the board, then fasten it to the joists using 2½" wood screws.

2. Install the remaining deck boards, keeping a ⅛" gap between the boards and extending the boards

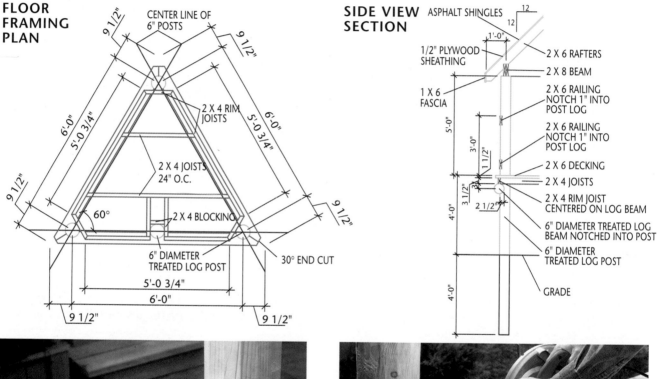

FLOOR FRAMING PLAN

CENTER LINE OF 6" POSTS
9½"
9½"
2 X 4 RIM JOISTS
6'-0"
5'-0 ¾"
5'-0 ¾"
6'-0"
9½"
2 X 4 JOISTS 24" O.C.
9½"
60°
2 X 4 BLOCKING
30° END CUT
6" DIAMETER TREATED LOG POST
5'-0 ¾"
6'-0"
9 1/2"
9 1/2"

SIDE VIEW SECTION

ASPHALT SHINGLES
12
12
1'-0"
1/2" PLYWOOD SHEATHING
2 X 6 RAFTERS
2 X 8 BEAM
1 X 6 FASCIA
2 X 6 RAILING NOTCH 1" INTO POST LOG
5'-0"
3'-0"
2 X 6 RAILING NOTCH 1" INTO POST LOG
1 1/2"
2 X 6 DECKING
2 X 4 JOISTS
3 1/2"
2 X 4 RIM JOIST CENTERED ON LOG BEAM
2 1/2"
6" DIAMETER TREATED LOG BEAM NOTCHED INTO POST
4'-0"
6" DIAMETER TREATED LOG POST
4'-0"
GRADE

D. *Cut rim joists to size and fasten them on top of the logs using spikes. Make sure the ends fit tightly together.*

E. *Fasten the deck boards to the joists, cut the two outside boards to fit, then cut the boards flush with the outside edges of the rim joists.*

past the rim joists. Drill pilot holes and install two screws per joist. Mark the last boards on each side to butt against the corner posts. Cut the boards at the marks using a jig saw and fasten them in place on the deck.

3. Snap a chalk line over the ends of the deck boards, flush with the outside edges of the rim joists. Cut the decking at the lines using a circular saw. Use a jig saw to cut places the circular saw can't reach.

Step F: Install the Railing

1. Measure from the top of the deck and mark the posts at 4" and 30½". Make a series of 1"-deep × 5½"-long cuts on the outsides of the posts above the marks using a reciprocating saw. Complete the notches using a hammer and chisel. Test-fit a piece of 2 × 6 lumber in the notches and make additional cuts as necessary.

2. Place a 2 × 6 rail in the notches on the right side, allowing the ends to extend past the posts. Clamp the rail in place. Place a scrap 2 × 6 in the notches on adjacent sides, then mark where they cross the first rail. Take down the rail and cut a 30° angle at the marks on both ends. Place the rail back in the notches and clamp it into place.

3. Cut a 30° angle on the end of a rail and set it in the notches on the left side. Butt the angled end tightly against the end of the first rail, then clamp it into place. Place a scrap 2 × 6 in the notch on the front side and mark where it crosses the left side rail. Take down the rail, cut a 30° angle at the mark, then

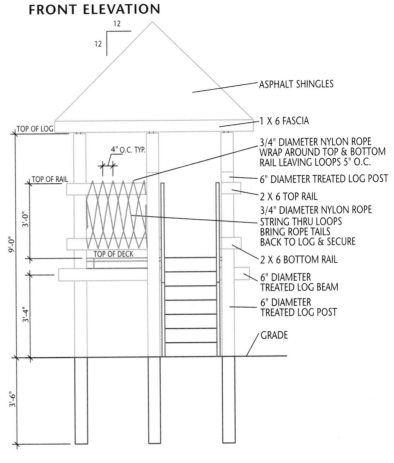

FRONT ELEVATION

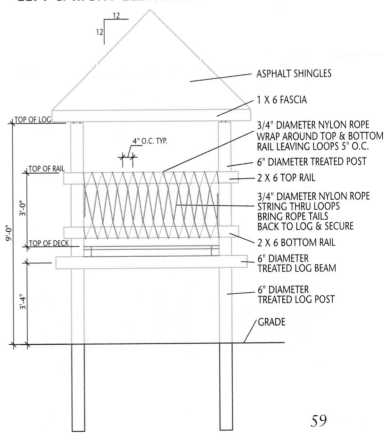

LEFT & RIGHT ELEVATION

F. *Set the rails in the notches, aligning them at the ends, then nail them to the posts using 16d nails.*

ROOF FRAMING PLAN

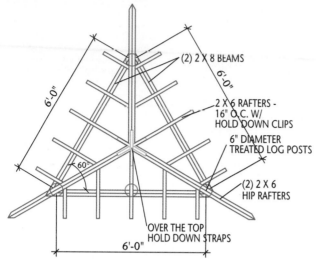

(2) 2 X 8 BEAMS

6'-0"

6'-0"

6'-0"

2 X 6 RAFTERS -
16" O.C. W/
HOLD DOWN CLIPS

6" DIAMETER
TREATED LOG POSTS

60°

(2) 2 X 6
HIP RAFTERS

OVER THE TOP
HOLD DOWN STRAPS

6'-0"

RAFTER TEMPLATE

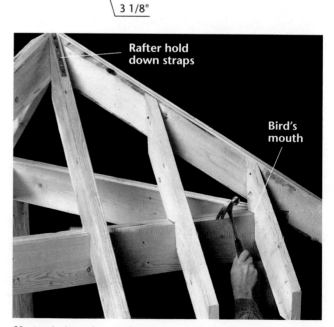

12

12

3'-10"

3"

4 5/8"

60°
END CUT
BOTH WAYS

3 THUS

3 1/8"

10 3/8"

60°

2'-9 5/8"

3"

4 5/8"

60°
END CUT

3 THUS
3 REVERSE

10 3/8"

3"

1'-8 1/2"

3"

4 5/8"

60°
END CUT

3 THUS
3 REVERSE

10 3/8"

3"

3 1/8"

HIP RAFTER TEMPLATE

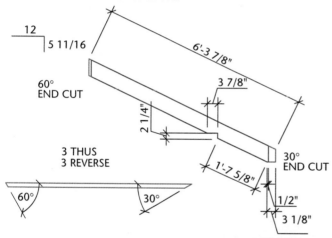

12

5 11/16

60°
END CUT

6'-3 7/8"

3 7/8"

2 1/4"

3 THUS
3 REVERSE

30°
END CUT

60°

30°

1'-7 5/8"

1/2"

3 1/8"

G. *Measure the distances between the corners, cut beams to those measurements with a 30° angle on each end, and toenail them to the posts.*

Rafter hold
down straps

Bird's
mouth

H. *Set the hip rafters in place, then install the rafters, fitting the bird's mouth over the beams.*

replace it in the notches and nail it into place.

4. Measure the distance between the end of the right side rail and left edge of the right front corner post. Measure the distance between the end of the left side rail and the right edge of the front middle post. Cut a 2 × 6 rail to each of those measurements.

5. Install the front rails, fitting the angled ends together with the side rails and keeping the square ends flush with the edges of posts. Repeat steps 2 through 5 to install the second row of railing.

Step G: Install the Roof Beams

1. Measure the distance between the centers of the three corner posts (each distance may be slightly different). Cut a 2 × 8 beam with a 30° angle on each end so the long end of the angles is at the center of the posts.

2. Place the beams on the corner posts so the inside edge of the beams is at the center of the posts. Butt the ends of the beams together and toenail them to the posts using 16d nails. Drive at least two toenails per beam.

3. Measure the distance between the outside edges of the beams and cut a beam to each of these three measurements with a 30° angle on each end so the short end of the angles is at the center of the posts. Place the beams outside the beams installed in the last step, butting the ends together. Facenail the beams together using 16d nails driven at a slight angle and toenail the beams to the posts.

Step H: Frame the Roof

1. Cut the hip rafters and rafters following the templates on the opposite page. Facenail the hip rafters together in pairs, flush at the ends, using 16d nails driven at a slight angle. Mark the hip rafters for the rafter locations 16" on-center, measuring from the top end.

2. Hang the hip rafters by placing the bird's mouth over the top of the roof beam corners and toenailing the top ends together using 8d nails. Toenail the bottom of the hip rafters to the beams.

3. Mark each beam at the centerpoint for a 2 × 6 rafter, then mark the other rafter locations 16" on center from the middle rafter.

4. Toenail the rafters in place with the bird's mouth cuts fitting over the beams using 8d nails. Reinforce the connections by installing rafter hold-down clips. Fasten the clips to the rafters and beams using 6d nails. Fasten the rafters to the hip rafters by toenailing 8d nails. Install hold down straps over the top of each hip rafter onto the rafter on the opposite side using 8d nails.

Step I: Install the Fascia & Sheathing

1. Measure the distance between the outside edges of the hip rafters on all three sides. Cut a 1 × 6 fascia trim board to each of those measurements with a 30° angle on each end. The inside edges of the angles should be the actual distances you measured, so the overall lengths of the fascia are slightly larger than

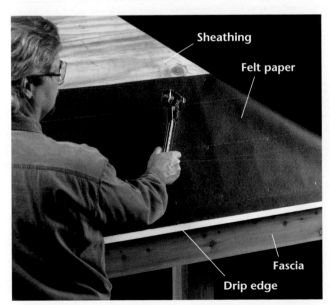

Labels: Sheathing · Felt paper · Fascia · Drip edge

I. *Cut plywood sheathing to fit over the roof, then nail drip edge along the bottom edges. Cover the sheathing and drip edge with felt paper.*

OVERHANG DETAIL

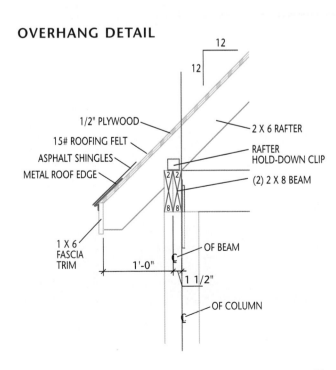

12 / 12

1/2" PLYWOOD
15# ROOFING FELT
ASPHALT SHINGLES
METAL ROOF EDGE
2 X 6 RAFTER
RAFTER HOLD-DOWN CLIP
(2) 2 X 8 BEAM
1 X 6 FASCIA TRIM
1'-0"
1 1/2"
OF BEAM
OF COLUMN

the measurements you took.

2. Nail the fascia over the rafter ends, flush with the top of the rafter face, so the inside angled edge of each fascia end is flush with the outside edge of the hip rafters. Butt the fascia ends together at the hip rafters. Secure the fascia to the rafters using 6d box nails.

3. Place a sheet of ½" plywood sheathing over the rafters so the bottom edge of the sheathing is flush with the outside edge of the fascia. Tack the sheathing in place. Snap a chalk line on both sides of the sheathing where it crosses the middle of the hip rafters. Take the sheathing down and cut it at the marks using a circular saw.

4. Set the sheathing back on the roof and fasten it in place using 6d box nails. Place a second sheet of sheathing above the first sheet. Snap a chalk line along the hip rafters. Remove the sheathing, cut it, then set it back into place and nail it. Do the same for the other two sides.

5. Install metal roof edge (drip edge) along the bottom edge of the sheathing. Use metal snips to cut the ends of the roof edge at a 30° angle to match the angle on the fascia. Nail drip edge on all three sides using galvanized roofing nails. **Note:** If you're using aluminum roof edge, use aluminum nails.

6. Staple felt roofing paper over the sheathing and drip edge, overlapping the paper at the ridges. Work from the bottom of the roof toward the peak, overlapping the lower row of paper by 2".

Step J: Shingle the Roof

1. Snap a chalk line 11½" from the front of the drip edge. Cut 6" off the end of a shingle using a utility knife. Position the shingle upside down on the roof so the bottom is flush with the chalk line. Mark and cut the first shingle to align with the side of the sheathing. Install the rest of the starter row the same way. Nail the shingles to the sheathing using ⅞" galvanized roofing nails.

2. Install the first row of shingles right side up, aligning the shingles with the bottom and side of the starter row. For the second row, overhang the first shingle by half a tab. Move each new row over half a tab, overlapping the shingles just above the tab slots. Measure up from the drip edge every few rows to make sure the rows are straight. Cut the shingles to fit the sides on the sheathing.

3. Cut three shingle caps per shingle. Snap a chalk line 6" on either side of the ridges. Install shingle caps over the ridges, flush with the chalk line. Fasten each cap with one nail on each side of the roof, 5½" from the finished edge and 1" from the side. Fasten the last shingle on top of the fort with a nail in each corner, then cover the nail heads with roofing cement.

Step K: Build & Install the Bridge

1. Measure down 42" from the top of the posts at the front of the bridge and 60" from the posts at the back of the bridge and make a mark. Drill ⅜" holes at the marks on the front face of the posts. Drill completely through the posts. Insert a ⅜ × 7" eye

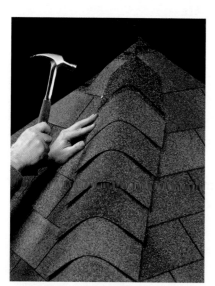

J. *Nail shingles on the roof, then cut shingle caps to fit over the ridges. Nail the caps over the ridges to complete the roof.*

K. *Run chains through the bridge boards, then connect the chains to the eye bolts on the posts.*

CHAIN THROUGH BRIDGE DECK

3 X 3 TREATED BRIDGE DECKING

5/16" CHAIN LINK

DRILL 3/4" DIAMETER HOLES THRU 3 X 3 DECKING FOR CHAIN

bolt with washer in each hole so the eye bolt is on the bridge side. Tighten a washer and nut on the eye bolts using a ratchet wrench.

2. Cut twenty 3 × 3 bridge decking boards at 42". Drill two ¾" holes through each board, 3" from the outside edges, centered from top to bottom.

3. Feed ⁵⁄₁₆" chain through the holes. One chain is for the holes on the left side of the boards, and a second chain is for the holes on the right side.

4. Attach a chain connector to the last link on both ends of the bridge chains. Attach the other end of the chain connectors to the eye bolts to set the bridge in place. Tighten the connectors using pliers.

Step L: Prepare the Stair Stringers

1. Cut two 2 × 12 stringers as shown below.

2. Use tape to mark the rise measurement on one leg of a framing square. Mark the run measurement with tape on the other leg. Place the square on the stringers with the tape marks flush to the edge. Outline the rise and run for each step. The top step is a 2 × 8. The remaining steps are 2 × 12s. Draw the tread outline along the bottom of each run line.

3. Attach riser supports to the stringers, flush with the bottom of each tread outline, by drilling ⁵⁄₃₂" pilot holes and inserting 1¼" screws.

Step M: Install the Stairs

1. Draw a line at the top of one stringer, 3½" from the edge of the 50° angle and parallel to the angle. Place the stringer inside the stair posts so the 3½"

STAIR SECTION

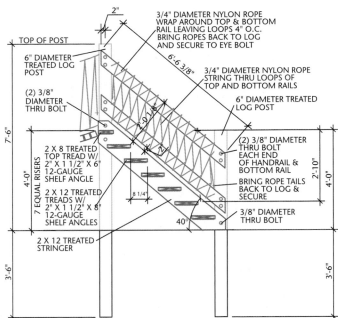

STAIR STRINGER

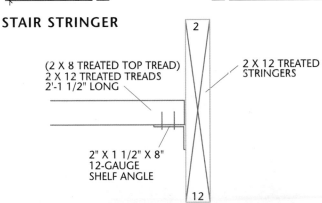

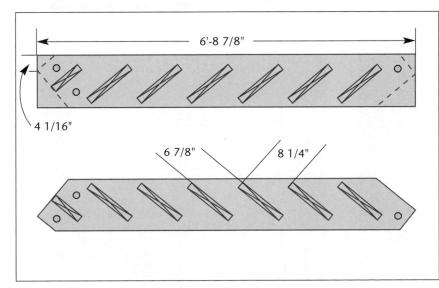

L. *Layout the stair stringers using a framing square, then attach riser supports.*

M. *Fasten the stringers to the posts using bolts, then attach treads to the riser supports on the stringers.*

STAIR STRINGER TO POST

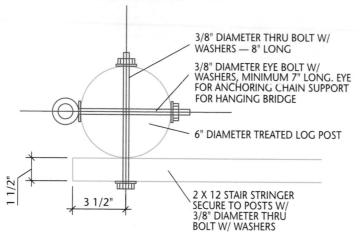

3/8" DIAMETER THRU BOLT W/ WASHERS — 8" LONG

3/8" DIAMETER EYE BOLT W/ WASHERS, MINIMUM 7" LONG. EYE FOR ANCHORING CHAIN SUPPORT FOR HANGING BRIDGE

6" DIAMETER TREATED LOG POST

1 1/2"

3 1/2"

2 X 12 STAIR STRINGER SECURE TO POSTS W/ 3/8" DIAMETER THRU BOLT W/ WASHERS

STAIR HANDRAIL TO POST

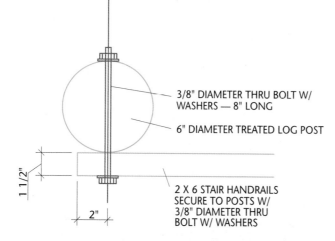

3/8" DIAMETER THRU BOLT W/ WASHERS — 8" LONG

6" DIAMETER TREATED LOG POST

1 1/2"

2"

2 X 6 STAIR HANDRAILS SECURE TO POSTS W/ 3/8" DIAMETER THRU BOLT W/ WASHERS

line is at the center of the post and the outline for the top tread is flush with the eye bolt for the bridge. Clamp the stringer to the posts.

2. Drill two ⅜" holes through the stringer at the line, one below and one above the tread location. Drill one hole at the bottom of the stringer. Drill the holes through the stringer and through the posts.

3. Insert a ⅜ × 8" bolt with washer through each hole in the stringer. Fasten a washer and nut on the end of each bolt at the outside of the posts and tighten using a ratchet wrench. Repeat steps 1 through 3 to install the second stringer.

4. Cut one 2 × 8 tread at 27". Cut six 2 × 12 treads at 27". Starting at the top of the stairs, set the 2 × 8 tread in place on the riser supports. Drill pilot holes through the supports into the bottom of the tread, then fasten using 1¼" screws. Attach the 2 × 12 treads the same way.

Step N: Attach the Stair Railings

1. Measure from the top of the stringers and mark the posts at the bottom and the top of the stairs at 2" and 24⅛".

2. Cut four 2 × 6 rails at 78⅜" with a 50° angle on each end. Draw a line 2" from each end, parallel to the 50° cuts.

3. Place the bottom rail against the inside face of the posts so the 2" lines align with the center of the posts and the bottom of the rail is flush with the

N. *Attach the rails to the posts on both sides of the stairs using bolts with washers and nuts.*

O. *Wrap rope around the rails 4" on center, then weave a third rope through the rope on the rails.*

2" measurements marked in step 1. Clamp the rail to the posts.

4. Drill two ⅜" holes at the 2" line on both ends of the rail. Drill completely through the posts.

5. Insert a ⅜ × 8" bolt with washer through the rail holes. Fasten washers and nuts on the end of the bolts and tighten using a ratchet wrench. Place plastic caps over the ends of the bolts in the posts.

6. Place the top rail under the 24⅛" mark on the posts. Repeat steps 3 to 5 to fasten it to the posts. Repeat these steps to fasten the rails to the other side of the stairs.

Step O: Install the Rope Rails

1. Measure down from the top of the posts at the front of the bridge and make a mark at 5" and 39". Measure from the top of the posts at the back of the bridge and make a mark at 23" and 57".

2. Drill a ⅜" hole through the posts at the center of each mark. Insert a ⅜ × 7" eye bolt with washer in each hole, fastening a washer and nut on each end. Insert ¾" nylon rope through each set of eye bolts on both sides of the bridge. Allow the rope to sag slightly to match the curve in your bridge. Fasten the rope by tying a knot under the eye bolts.

3. Drill a ⅜" pilot hole in the posts at the front and the back of the bridge about three quarters of the way down between the rope rails installed in the

last step. Insert a 4" eye bolt in the holes.

4. Fasten a rope in an eye bolt by tying a knot, then wrap the rope around the top and bottom rope rails. Space the rope on the rails 4" on-center, fastening the rope to the rails by tying knots. When you reach the post at the opposite side, attach the rope to the eye bolt by tying a knot. Do this on both sides of the bridge.

5. Lightly make a mark every 4" on the rails on the stairs and fort. Make sure the marks on the bottom rails are offset 2½" from the marks on the top rails.

6. Drill pilot holes and insert eye bolts in the posts next to each rail. Fasten rope in an eye bolt, then wrap the rope around the rail, overlapping the 4" marks. Keep the rope fairly snug against the rail. Fasten the end of the rope to the eye bolt on the opposite side. Do this for each rail.

7. Drill pilot holes and insert an eye bolt in the posts at the bottom and the top of the stairs, fairly close to the bottom rail. Fasten a rope to an eye bolt, then weave the other end of the rope between the ropes on the top and bottom rails. When you reach the opposite post, fasten the rope to the eye bolt. Do this for each set of rails on the stairs and fort.

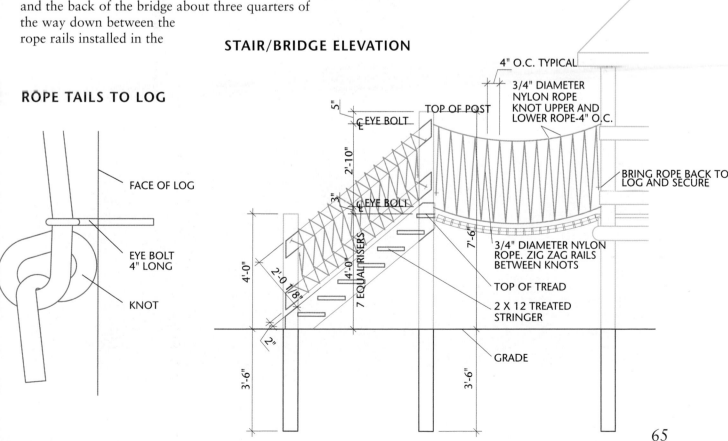

ROPE TAILS TO LOG

STAIR/BRIDGE ELEVATION

65

Open-air Arbor

This child-sized arbor offers the perfect open-air play place for children. Two of the walls have low shelves where young kids can put their toys or older kids can sit. The third wall contains the entrance, while the fourth wall is solid. Using lattice for the walls allows children to have some privacy while they play, yet it doesn't completely close the structure off to nice summer breezes. The canvas fabric on the roof brings a splash of color to the arbor in addition to providing a screen from the sun. The plans call for 12" diameter footings, although 10" footings will also work.

Kids can bring their toys or lawn furniture into the arbor for playtime. They can also use it as a retreat, a place to sit by themselves and read a book. It's extremely versatile and can be used for almost any type of play or recreation.

The arbor is relatively simple to build and the lattice walls are easy to construct. While you can substitute wood lattice instead of vinyl, vinyl is much easier to work with and doesn't chip or break apart when you cut it. Vinyl lattice looks just like wood, but it doesn't require any painting or other maintenance.

MATERIAL LIST

DESCRIPTION	QTY./SIZE	MATERIAL
Support System		
Concrete tube forms	4 @ 12"-diameter	
Gravel	4"-deep per hole (if needed)	
Concrete	Depth per local code	3500 PSI concrete
J-bolts, washers, nuts	4	
Wall Framing		
Corner posts	4 @ 6'-0"	4 × 4 treated
Post base anchors	4 with nails	Simpson PBS44A adj. post base
Top rail	1 @ 8'-0"	2 × 4 treated
Opening trim/studs	3 @ 8'-0"	2 × 4 treated
Bottom rail	4 @ 8'-0"	2 × 6 treated
Bottom rail	4 @ 8'-0"	2 × 4 treated
Stops	18 @ 8'-0"	¾ × ¾ S4S cedar
Shelves	2 @ 8'-0"	2 × 10 treated
Shelf supports	4 @ 8'-0"	2 × 4 treated
Stakes	1 @ 8'-0"	2 × 4 treated
Galvanized carriage bolts	8 @ ½ × 4"	Post base anchor to post

DESCRIPTION	QTY./SIZE	MATERIAL
Roof Framing		
Tie beams	2 @ 10'-0"	4 × 6 treated
Rafters	4 @ 10'-0"	2 × 4 treated
Cross strips	6 @ 10'-0"	2 × 2 treated
Roof panels	3 @ 13'-0"	Colored canvas
Molding	6 @ 8'	¼ × 1⅛" molding
Connectors	4 with nails	Simpson L50 - beam to post
Galvanized wood screws	40 @ 2½"	Rafters to beams, cross strips to rafters
Exterior Finishes		
Lattice	2 @ 3'-7½" × 5'-7"	Manufactured panels
Lattice	4 @ 3'-7" × 1'-4"	Manufactured panels
Lattice	2 @ 2'-3½" × 5'-4"	Manufactured panels
Miscellaneous		
Galvanized finish nails	16d - 3 pounds	Lumber to lumber
Galvanized box nails	8d - 2 pounds	Lumber to lumber
Galvanized common nails	16d, 3d - 1 pound each	Lumber to lumber
Galvanized wood screws	80 @ 2"	Lumber to lumber

CUTTING LIST

PART	QTY.	SIZE
Framing		
Corner posts	4	4 × 4 × 72"
Tie beams	2	4 × 6 × 120" w/45° angle on ends
Rafters	4	2 × 4 × 120" w/45° angle on ends
Cross strips	6	2 × 2 × 120" w/45° angle on ends
Right Side Wall		
Bottom rails	2	2 × 6 × 89"
Center stud	1	2 × 4 × 62½"
Cedar stops*	8	¾ × ¾ × 62½"
Lattice panels**	2	43½ × 67"
Front Wall		
Top rail	1	2 × 4 × 89"
Cedar stops*	8	¾ × ¾ × 66½"
Opening trim	2	2 × 4 × 72"
Bottom rails	2	2 × 6 × 28"
Lattice panels**	2	27½ × 70"

PART	QTY.	SIZE
Back and Left Side Walls		
Shelf supports	4	2 × 4 × 43¾"
Shelf supports	2	2 × 4 × 89"
Bottom rails	4	2 × 4 × 89"
Wall studs	2	2 × 4 × 13½"
Cedar stops*	8	¾ × ¾ × 13½"
Cedar stops*	8	¾ × ¾ × 10"
Lattice panels**	4	16½ × 43½"
Shelves		
Shelves	2	2 × 10 × 92½"
Roof Panels		
Canvas roof panels	3	30 × 110"
Molding	6	¼ × 1⅛ × 8"

Note: Cut all lumber to size and paint before starting project

*Actual cedar stop dimensions are approximately 1 × 1"

**Lattice panels are cut slightly smaller than the actual size of the walls to give ⅛" of space on each side and to make installation easier.

Note: When working with treated lumber, hot-dipped galvanized or stainless steel nails, fasteners, and fittings are recommended.

HOW TO BUILD AN OPEN-AIR ARBOR

Step A: Dig the Concrete Footings

Note: Refer to pages 28 to 29 for additional information on laying out and pouring concrete footings.

1. Set up batter boards in a square pattern and run mason's lines to form a 92½ × 92½" square. Keep the mason's lines tight. Measure diagonally between the corners and make any necessary adjustments until the diagonals are equal to one another.

2. Drive a stake in the ground at each corner. Measure 27" from the right and left corners on the front side and make a mark on a piece of tape attached to the mason's line. Drive a stake into the ground at each of these marks for the braces. Take down the mason's lines.

3. Dig holes at the brace locations on the front side of the arbor using a posthole digger. Make the holes at least 24" deep. **Note:** These holes will not be filled until Step H.

4. Dig holes at the corners for the concrete forms. Use the stake locations as the center for the holes. Dig the holes slightly larger than the 12"-diameter footings and to a depth that extends below the frost line and meets local building code requirements. Be sure to add an additional 4" to the depth for the gravel base.

Step B: Pour the Footings

1. Add 4" of gravel to each hole and set the concrete forms in place. Restring the mason's lines.

Attach a line level on the mason's lines and adjust the lines until they're level. Confirm that the forms are centered under the corner points and make adjustments if necessary.

2. Mark one of the forms approximately 2" above ground level. Measure the distance from the mark on the form and the mason's line. Mark that same measurement on the three remaining forms. For example, if the first form is marked 12" below the mason's line, then all forms must be marked 12" below the line.

3. Wrap a sheet of paper around each form at the marks, then draw a line around the outside of the form. Cut the forms using a handsaw or reciprocating saw. Place the forms back in their respective holes.

4. Level the forms and secure them with packed soil around the outside. Fill each form with concrete. Level the concrete using a 2 × 4 on-edge.

5. Insert a J-bolt in the concrete at the center of each form, keeping the top of the bolt ¾ to 1" above the concrete. Make sure the bolt is plumb using a level. Use a plumb bob to align the bolts directly under the corners on the mason's lines. Once each bolt is placed, smooth the concrete around the bolts. Allow the concrete to harden before continuing.

Step C: Set the Posts

Note: Refer to pages 30 to 31 for additional information on setting posts.

A. *Set up batter boards and run mason's lines. Mark the corners and brace locations with stakes, then dig the holes.*

B. *Fill each form with concrete, level the top with a 2 × 4, then insert a J-bolt at the center of the form.*

C. *Tack the corner post into the anchor, plumb adjacent sides, brace it on two sides, then fasten the post to the anchor.*

1. Cut away the concrete forms at ground level using a utility knife.

2. Place a straight 2 × 4 board against the J-bolts on the two right side footings. Draw a reference line along the bolt side edge of the stud across the top of the concrete on both footings. Repeat this step for the footings on the left side.

3. Place a post base anchor on each footing, centering each anchor over the J-bolt. Position the anchors so they're square to the reference lines, using a framing square. Place a washer and nut on the end of each J-bolt and tighten it using a ratchet wrench.

4. Center a 4 × 4 × 72" corner post on an anchor. Tack the corner post in place using an 8d galvanized nail. Fasten two temporary braces to adjacent sides of the post to hold it in place. Use a level to plumb adjacent sides of the post, adjusting the braces as necessary until the post is perfectly plumb.

5. Finish nailing the anchor to the corner post using 16d common nails. Drill two ½" holes through the post at the anchor hole locations. Insert a ½ × 4" galvanized carriage bolt through each hole. Tighten a washer and nut on the end of each bolt using a ratchet wrench. Set the other three posts the same way.

Step D: Install the Tie Beams

1. Place a tie beam on top of the right side corner posts. Position the beam so the top edge extends 12" past the outside edge of the corner posts on both

ROOF PLAN

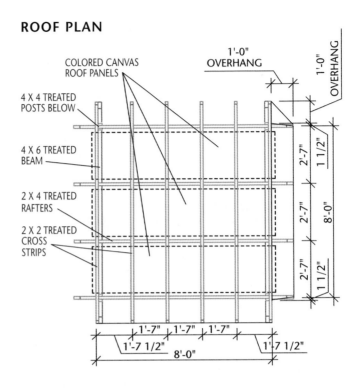

COLORED CANVAS ROOF PANELS

4 X 4 TREATED POSTS BELOW

4 X 6 TREATED BEAM

2 X 4 TREATED RAFTERS

2 X 2 TREATED CROSS STRIPS

1'-0" OVERHANG

1'-0" OVERHANG

2'-7"

1 1/2"

2'-7"

8'-0"

2'-7"

1 1/2"

1'-7" 1'-7" 1'-7"

1'-7 1/2"   1'-7 1/2"

8'-0"

ends. Align the outside edge of the beam with the outside edges of the posts. Toenail the beam into place using 8d galvanized box nails.

2. Secure the beam to the posts using galvanized connectors. Place the connectors on the inside face of each post and along the bottom edge of the beam,

D. *Place the tie beam on the corner posts, keeping an equal distance on the overhangs. Toenail the beam in place, then fasten the galvanized connectors (inset).*

E. *Place the rafters on the tie beams 31" on-center. Nail the rafters into place.*

then fasten them in place using 8d galvanized nails.

3. Repeat steps 1 and 2 to install the tie beam on the left side.

Step E: Attach the Rafters

1. Place the first rafter on-edge across the tie beams so the ends of the rafter overhang the beams by 12". Center the rafter over the front corner posts.

2. Toenail 8d galvanized nails through the side of the rafter where it crosses the tie beams to fasten the rafter into place. Repeat this process to fasten a rafter into place over the back corner posts.

3. Fasten the remaining two rafters on the tie beams 31" on-center, using 8d galvanized nails.

Step F: Attach the Cross Strips

1. Place a cross strip over the rafters. Keep the outside edge of the cross strip flush with the outside edge of the tie beam. Overhang the rafters by 12" to align the cross beam with the ends of the tie beam. Drill two ³⁄₃₂" pilot holes in the cross strip where it crosses the rafters and insert 2½" galvanized wood screws. Align a cross strip with the tie beam on the opposite side of the arbor using the same method.

2. Place a cross strip so its center is 19½" from the outside edge of each end cross strip and fasten them to the rafters by drilling pilot holes and inserting wood screws.

3. Fasten the two remaining cross strips to the

rafters 19" on-center from the rafters installed in the last step.

Step G: Build the Right Side Wall

1. Mark the vertical center on the inside faces of the right side corner posts. Measure back from the center mark half the thickness of the lattice panels and make another mark at the top and bottom of both posts. Snap a chalk line between the last two marks. Place the chalk line on the marks at the top of both posts and snap a line on the bottom of the tie beam.

2. Place a 62½" cedar stop on the corner posts so the outside edge is flush with the chalk line and the top end is butted against the beam. Drill ³⁄₃₂" pilot holes and fasten the stop to the posts using 8d galvanized box nails.

3. Set a 2 × 6 bottom rail directly under the stops, between the posts, with its outside edge flush with the chalk line. Toenail the rail to the posts using 16d galvanized nails.

4. From the outside edge of the back corner post, measure 47¼" along the tie beam and the bottom rail and make a mark. Set the center stud in front of the marks, flush with the outside edge of the tie beam, and toenail it in place. Place a stop on both faces of the stud so the outside edges of the stops are aligned with the chalk line on the tie beam and the outside edge of the bottom rail. Drill ³⁄₃₂" pilot holes and fasten the stops with 2" galvanized wood screws.

F. *Fasten the cross strips perpendicular to the rafters by drilling pilot holes and inserting wood screws.*

G. *Set the lattice panels against the stops and bottom rail, then set the outer stops over the panels and fasten them in place.*

H. *Fasten 2 x 4 stakes at the end of the bottom rails to anchor the front walls at the opening.*

5. Measure the distance between the stops on the corner posts and the stops on the center stud. Cut four stops to that measurement. Install two of those stops in place along the chalk line on the bottom side of the tie beam.

6. Place the 43½ × 67" panels against the stops and bottom rail. Tack the panels in place against the stops under the tie beam.

7. Install the outer stops over the panels. Drill ³⁄₃₂" pilot holes through the outer stops and the lattice, then insert 2" wood screws. Also secure the outer stops to the posts and tie beam.

8. Set the bottom rails in place and attach them to the inner bottom rails using 16d galvanized common nails.

Step H: Build the Front Wall

1. Fasten the 2 × 4 top rail under the rafter, flush with the edge of the corner posts, using 8d nails.

2. Repeat Step G, number 1 to mark the location of the outside stops on the corner beams. Install the stops at the marks.

3. Butt a bottom rail against the corner post on each side, directly beneath the stops, flush with the chalk line. Toenail the rails to the posts using 16d nails.

4. Mark the location of the stops on the opening trim by locating the center of the board and measuring over half the thickness of the lattice panels. Measure 33" from the outside of each post and

mark the top rail. Set the opening trim at the outside of each mark, flush with the outside edges of the top rail, and toenail it into place. Facenail the bottom end of the trim to the bottom rails, keeping the rails flush with the mark for the stops, using 16d nails.

SECTION VIEWS

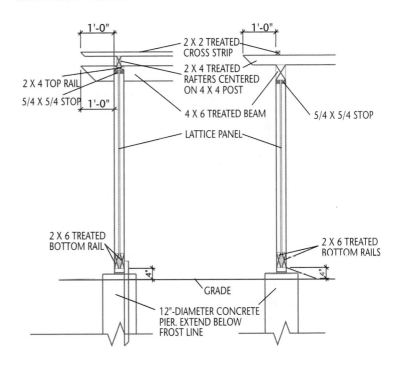

RIGHT SIDE ELEVATION

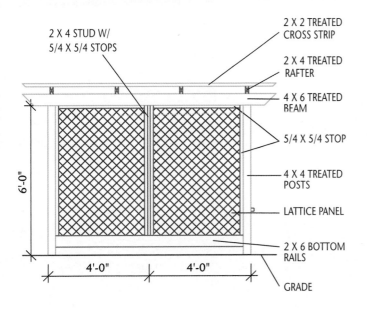

FRONT ELEVATION

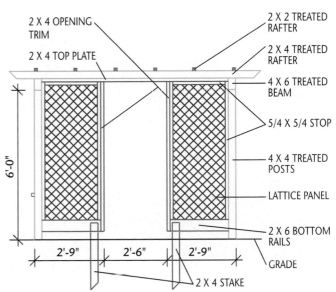

5. Install a stop on the outside face of each opening trim piece, flush with the stop marks. The stops sit on top of the bottom rails.

6. Measure the distance between the stops on the corner posts and the stops on the opening trim. Cut four stops to this measurement, then install a stop to the underside of the top rail on each side of the opening trim, flush with the edges of the vertical stops.

7. Place the lattice panels against the stops and bottom rails and tack them into place. Place the outer stops and bottom rails against the panels and fasten them into place.

8. Place a 2 × 4 stake at the end of each bottom rail to fit in the holes dug in Step A. Make sure the stakes cover the bottom rails by at least 4". Plumb the stakes, then fasten them to the rails using 8d nails. Backfill the holes around the stakes with dirt.

Step I: Build the Left Side and Back Walls

1. Repeat Step G, number 1 to mark the location of the stops on the back and left side corner posts.

2. Measure from the bottom of the corner posts and make a mark at 7½" and 21". Toenail a bottom rail on the corner posts so the top of the rail is flush with the 7½" mark and the outside of the board is flush with the mark for the stops. Do this on the left side and back posts.

3. Mark the locations of the stops on the wall studs. Measuring from the outside of a corner post, mark the bottom rails at 48". Center a wall stud on the bottom rail at the mark so the stop marks on the

stud are aligned with the edge of the bottom rail. Toenail the stud to the rail. Do this on both sides.

4. Toenail a 43¾" shelf support to the corner post below the 21" mark and to the wall stud, flush with the top. Align the outside edge of the shelf support with the stop marks on the corner post and wall stud. Fasten a shelf support on both sides of the wall stud on both the left and back sides.

5. Place an 89" shelf support over the supports installed in the last step. Align the 89" supports with the top and ends of the shorter supports and fasten together using 2½" galvanized wood screws.

6. Fasten the 10" stops to the corner posts and wall studs. Tack the lattice panels in place against the stops and bottom rails.

7. Nail the outer bottom rails in place. Install the 13½" stops over the lattice panels at the corner posts and wall studs. Measure the distance between the stops on the posts and the studs, and cut four stops at that measurement. Install those stops over the lattice panels, flush with the top of the shelf supports.

Step J: Install the Shelves

1. Notch the ends of the shelves to fit around the corner posts following the Corner Detail illustration. Miter cut a 45° angle on the end of each shelf leading away from the notch.

2. Set the shelves in place, making sure the angles fit tightly together. Fasten the shelves in place by driving 16d finish nails through the shelves into the shelf supports.

BACK ELEVATION

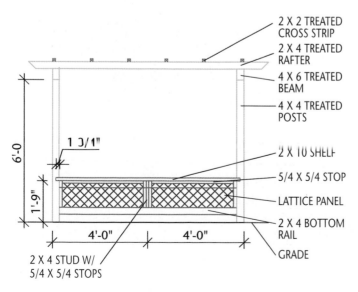

LEFT SIDE ELEVATION

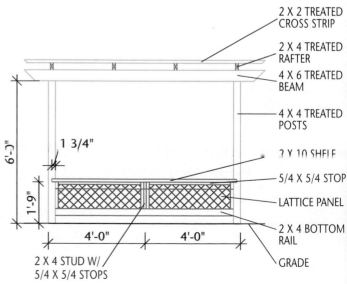

Step K: Installs the Roof Panels

1. Fold over the edges of the canvas panels by ¼", then fold them again another ¼" and sew the edges.

2. Drape the panels over the cross strips between the rafters. Keep an equal overhang of 12" on each end. Allow the panels to sag between the cross strips.

3. Place the molding over the cross strips, 12" from either end, covering the roof panels. Fasten the molding to the cross strips using 3d nails.

SECTION AT SHELF

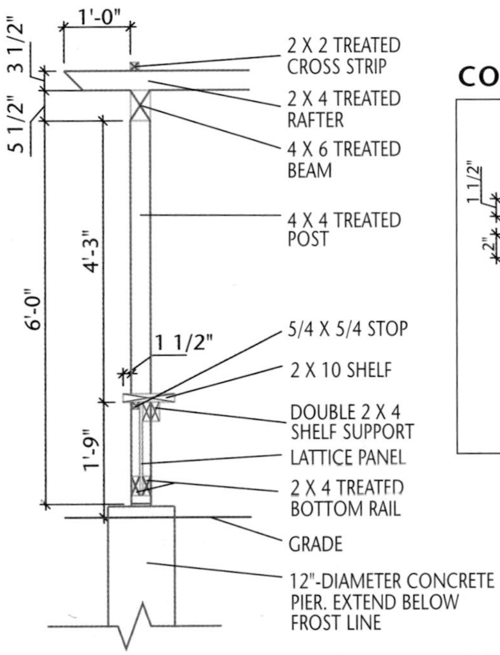
1'-0"
3 1/2"
5 1/2"
4'-3"
6'-0"
1'-9"
1 1/2"
2 X 2 TREATED CROSS STRIP
2 X 4 TREATED RAFTER
4 X 6 TREATED BEAM
4 X 4 TREATED POST
5/4 X 5/4 STOP
2 X 10 SHELF
DOUBLE 2 X 4 SHELF SUPPORT
LATTICE PANEL
2 X 4 TREATED BOTTOM RAIL
GRADE
12"-DIAMETER CONCRETE PIER. EXTEND BELOW FROST LINE

CORNER DETAIL

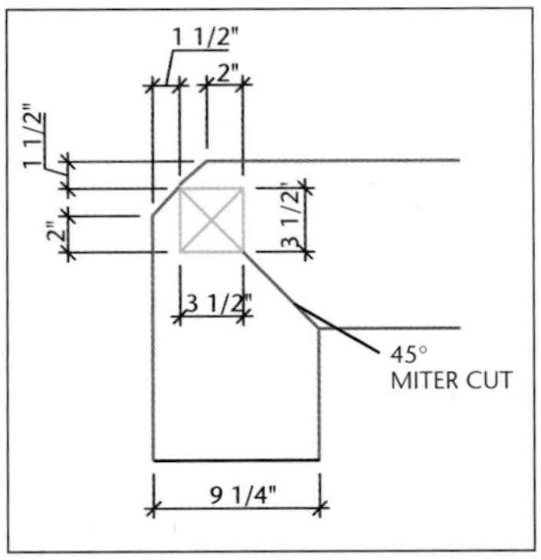
1 1/2"
2"
1 1/2"
2"
3 1/2"
3 1/2"
45° MITER CUT
9 1/4"

FLOOR PLAN

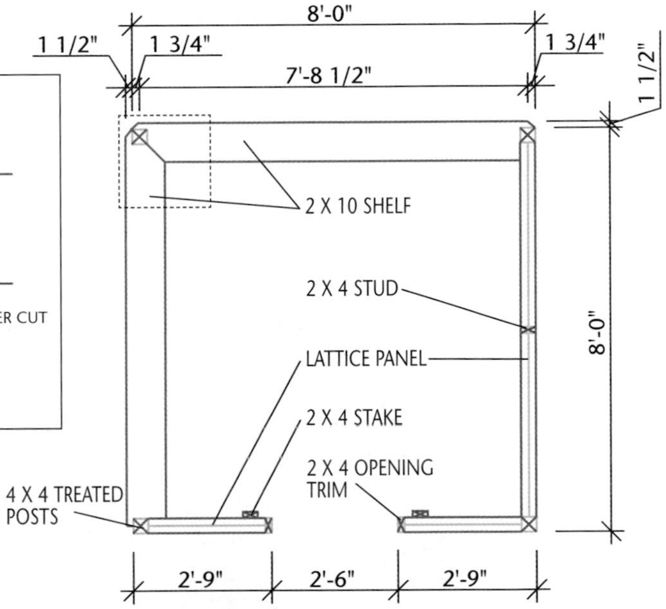
8'-0"
1 1/2"
1 3/4"
1 3/4"
7'-8 1/2"
1 1/2"
2 X 10 SHELF
2 X 4 STUD
LATTICE PANEL
2 X 4 STAKE
2 X 4 OPENING TRIM
4 X 4 TREATED POSTS
8'-0"
2'-9"
2'-6"
2'-9"

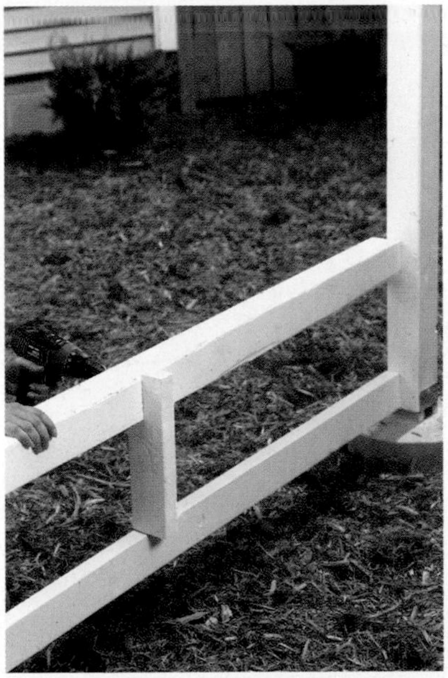

I. *Install a double shelf support that ties into the corner posts and center stud. Place stops between the supports and the bottom rails.*

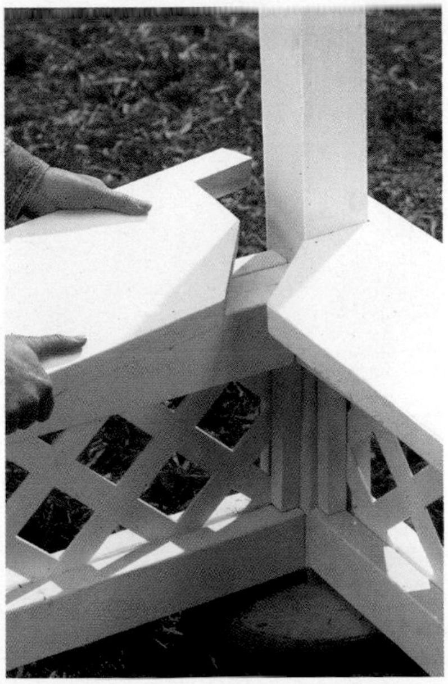

J. *Notch the ends of the shelves, cut a 45° angle in the end, then set them in place over the shelf supports.*

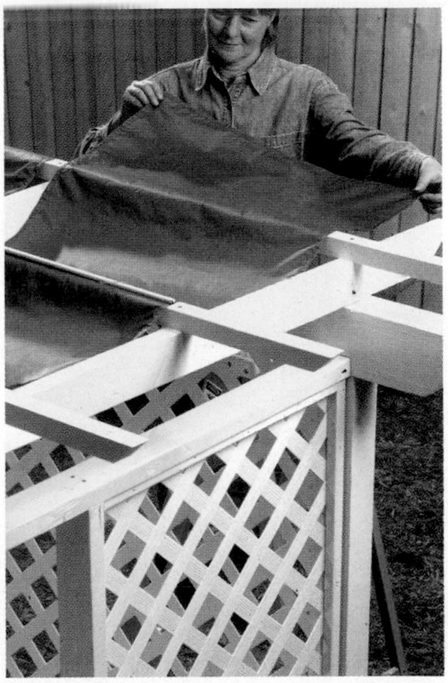

K. *Place the canvas roof panels over the cross strips, then attach the molding to hold the canvas in place.*

Clubhouse

A clubhouse is a proven favorite for children of all ages. This clubhouse features several fun components to keep kids engaged, including a sandbox, trapdoor with rope, open deck, and enclosed play structure.

The floor of the clubhouse sits eight feet off the ground. The elevated structure adds to the excitement of play, especially when kids can escape by lifting the trapdoor and sliding down the rope. The clubhouse features openings on all four sides as well as openings on the gable ends to allow for sunlight and air circulation. The openings are at safe heights to prevent injuries.

While the clubhouse is not watertight, it does have a shingled roof to protect against wind and rain. The deck gives children an open air area to enjoy while playing. The sandbox underneath the deck maximizes space and offers yet another way for kids to have fun.

The construction of the clubhouse is fairly straightforward with everything built on six 4 × 4 posts. It's sure to be the focus of your backyard and provide years of fun for your family.

MATERIAL LIST

DESCRIPTION	QTY./SIZE	MATERIAL
Support System		
Posts	4 @ 12'-0"	4 × 4 treated
Posts	2 @ 9'-0"	4 × 4 treated
Cross bridging	2 @ 8'-0"	2 × 4 treated
Baseboard	3 @ 6'-0"	2 × 12 treated
Baseboard	2 @ 8'-0"	2 × 12 treated
Floor Framing		
Rim joists	8 @ 6'-0"	2 × 6 treated
Rim joists	4 @ 8'-0"	2 × 6 treated
Joists	2 @ 8'-0"	2 × 6 treated
Trapdoor header	1 @ 4'-0"	2 × 6 treated
Trapdoor stop	1 @ 8'-0"	2 × 4 treated
Trapdoor nailer	1 @ 4'-0"	2 × 4 treated
Decking	17 @ 6'-0"	2 × 6 treated
Joist hangers	8 w/nails	Simpson U26
Rim joist hangers	16 w/nails	Simpson HUC26-2
Wall Framing		
Purlins	3 @ 10'-0"	2 × 4 SPF construction grade #2
Door jambs	3 @ 8'-0"	2 × 4 SPF construction grade #2
Top plates	4 @ 10'-0"	2 × 4 SPF construction grade #2
Studs	2 @ 8'-0"	2 × 4 SPF construction grade #2
Gable studs	1 @ 4'-0"	2 × 4 SPF construction grade #2
Roof Framing		
Rafters	4 @ 8'-0"	2 × 6 SPF construction grade #2
Ridge	1 @ 6'-0"	2 × 8 SPF construction grade #2
Gable stud	1 @ 6'-0"	2 × 4 SPF construction grade #2
Rope supports	1 @ 4'-0"	2 × 6 SPF construction grade #2
Roof sheathing	2 @ 4 × 8'	½" APA-rated plywood
Hold down clips	8 w/nails	Simpson H3
Sandbox		
Frame	3 @ 8'-0"	2 × 4 treated
Side plates, braces	1 @ 8'-0"	2 × 6 treated
Stops/mid support	4 @ 8'-0"	2 × 2 treated
Screen	1 @ 3'-7½" × 4'-9"	8-gauge wire 1½" sq. opening
Hinge	2 w/screws	3" × 3" exterior-grade hinge
Handle	1 w/screws	6" door pull
Latch	2 w/screws	Industrial gate latch
Exterior Finishes		
Siding	18 @ 10'-0"	1 × 8 tongue & groove V-joint cedar
Fascia	2 @ 6'-0"	1 × 6 S4S cedar
Roof		
Shingles	64 sq. feet	Minimum 250# per square
Roofing felt	64 sq. feet	15# roofing felt
Metal roof edge	4 @ 8'-0"	Galv. metal
Galvanized roofing nails	⅞" – ½ lb.	Shingles to roof sheathing

DESCRIPTION	QTY./SIZE	MATERIAL
Ladder		
Stringer	2 @ 6'-0"	2 × 4 S4S cedar
Rungs	3 @ 1'-10"	¾" diameter galvanized pipe
Ladder ends	1 @ 4'-0"	2 × 4 S4S cedar
Stairs		
Stringer	2 @ 10'-0"	2 × 10 treated
Treads	4 @ 8'-0"	2 × 6 treated
Tread clips	24	1½" × 1½" × 4" 16-gauge angle
Angle brackets	2 w/4d joist hanger nails	Stringers to deck
Galvanized lag screws	156 @ ¼" × 1¼"	Angle to treads
Stair footing	1 @ 4'-0"	2 × 12 treated
Deck and Stair Railing		
Top rail	3 @ 10'-0"	2 × 6 S4S cedar
Top rail	1 @ 6'-0"	2 × 6 S4S cedar
Balusters	54 @ 4'-0"	2 × 2 S4S cedar
Railing posts	3 @ 4'-0"	4 × 4 S4S cedar

DESCRIPTION	QTY./SIZE	MATERIAL
Deck and Stair Railing (cont.)		
Carriage bolts	6 @ ⅜" × 5"	Railing posts to stringers
Nailer	1 @ 6'-0"	2 × 2 treated
Deck fascia	1 @ 6'-0"	2 × 8 S4S cedar
Deck fascia	2 @ 8'-0"	2 × 8 S4S cedar
Miscellaneous		
Trap door hinge	1 @ 18"	2" piano hinge
Galvanized box nails	16d – 4 lbs.	Lumber to lumber
Galvanized common nails	10d – 2 lbs.	Joist hangers to joists
Box nails	6d – 1 lb.	Sheathing to lumber
Galvanized finish nails	6d – ½ lb.	Trim
Coated common nails	4d – ½ lb.	Siding to framing
Galvanized wood screws	250 @ 2½"	Decking to framing, trap door

CUTTING LIST

PART	QTY.	SIZE
Base Framing		
Corner posts	4	4 × 4 × 139½"
Corner posts	2	4 × 4 × 107"
Baseboards	2	2 × 12 × 96"
Baseboards	3	2 × 12 × 69"
Floor Framing		
Rim joists	4	2 × 6 × 62"
Rim joists	4	2 × 6 × 41"
Joists	2	42"
Trapdoor headers	2	2 × 6 × 19½"
Trapdoor stops	2	2 × 4 × 19½"
Trapdoor stops	2	2 × 4 × 19"
Trapdoor nailers	2	2 × 4 × 19"
Wall Framing		
Corner studs	4	2 × 4 × 43½"
Top plates	2	2 × 4 × 48"
Top plates	2	2 × 4 × 62"
Top plates	2	2 × 4 × 69"
Top plates	2	2 × 4 × 41"
Door jambs	4	2 × 4 × 43½"
Door purlin	1	2 × 4 × 24"
Purlins	2	2 × 4 × 14½"
Purlins	2	2 × 4 × 59"
Purlins	4	2 × 4 × 41"
Door jambs	6	2 × 4 × 8"
Roof		
Ridge board	1	2 × 8 × 69"
Fascia boards	2	1 × 6 × 69"
Rope supports	2	2 × 6 × 20"
Siding		
Tongue-and-groove boards	36	1 × 8 × 53½"
Door sill	1	2 × 8 × 24"

PART	QTY.	SIZE
Deck		
Rim joists	4	2 × 6 × 62"
Rim joists	4	2 × 6 × 41½"
Joists	2	2 × 6 × 42½"
Deck fascia	2	2 × 8 × 69"
Deck fascia	2	2 × 8 × 51½"
Stairs		
Stair footing	1	2 × 12 × 36"
Treads	12	2 × 6 × 24"
Balasters	22	2 × 2 × 38½"
Deck Rails		
Posts	2	4 × 4 × 42¼" with a 45° angle on one end
Post	1	4 × 4 × 41¼" with a 45° angle on each end
Balusters	47	2 × 2 × 41¼" with a 45° angle on each end
Balusters	13	2 × 2 × 23" with a 45° angle on one end
Rail	1	2 × 6 × 69"
Rail	2	2 × 6 × 50"
Baluster nailer	1	2 × 2 × 69"
Sandbox		
Side plates	2	2 × 6 × 41½"
Sandbox braces	4	2 × 6 × 3"
Cover frames	2	2 × 4 × 57"
Cover frames	2	2 × 4 × 46½"
Stops	2	2 × 2 × 57"
Stops	3	2 × 2 × 40½"
Stamped metal screen cover	1	57 × 43½"
Ladder		
Ladder stringers	2	2 × 4 × 68"
Ladder ends	2	2 × 4 × 21"

Note: When working with treated lumber, hot-dipped galvanized or stainless steel nails, fasteners, and fittings are recommended.

FRONT ELEVATION

REAR ELEVATION

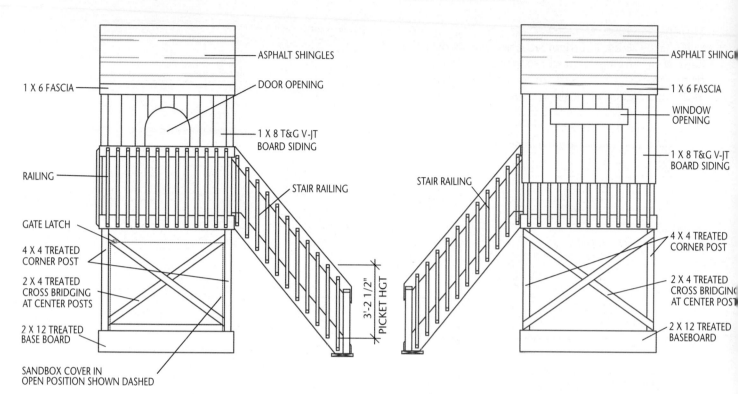

ASPHALT SHINGLES

1 X 6 FASCIA

DOOR OPENING

1 X 8 T&G V-JT BOARD SIDING

RAILING

STAIR RAILING

GATE LATCH

4 X 4 TREATED CORNER POST

2 X 4 TREATED CROSS BRIDGING AT CENTER POSTS

2 X 12 TREATED BASE BOARD

SANDBOX COVER IN OPEN POSITION SHOWN DASHED

3'-2 1/2" PICKET HGT

ASPHALT SHING

1 X 6 FASCIA

WINDOW OPENING

1 X 8 T&G V-JT BOARD SIDING

STAIR RAILING

4 X 4 TREATED CORNER POST

2 X 4 TREATED CROSS BRIDGIN AT CENTER POST

2 X 12 TREATED BASEBOARD

BUILDING SECTION

RIGHT ELEVATION

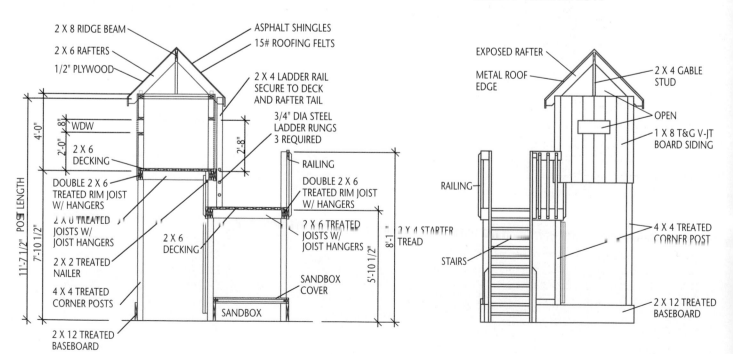

2 X 8 RIDGE BEAM

2 X 6 RAFTERS

1/2" PLYWOOD

ASPHALT SHINGLES

15# ROOFING FELTS

2 X 4 LADDER RAIL SECURE TO DECK AND RAFTER TAIL

3/4" DIA STEEL LADDER RUNGS 3 REQUIRED

WDW

2 X 6 DECKING

DOUBLE 2 X 6 TREATED RIM JOIST W/ HANGERS

2 X 6 TREATED JOISTS W/ JOIST HANGERS

2 X 2 TREATED NAILER

4 X 4 TREATED CORNER POSTS

2 X 12 TREATED BASEBOARD

2 X 6 DECKING

RAILING

DOUBLE 2 X 6 TREATED RIM JOIST W/ HANGERS

2 X 6 TREATED JOISTS W/ JOIST HANGERS

SANDBOX COVER

SANDBOX

2 X 4 STARTER TREAD

4'-0"

8"

2'-0"

2'-8"

11'-7 1/2" POST LENGTH

7'-10 1/2"

5'-10 1/2"

8'-1"

EXPOSED RAFTER

METAL ROOF EDGE

2 X 4 GABLE STUD

OPEN

1 X 8 T&G V-JT BOARD SIDING

RAILING

STAIRS

4 X 4 TREATED CORNER POST

2 X 12 TREATED BASEBOARD

HOW TO BUILD A CLUBHOUSE

Step A: Assemble the Base

1. Place the left and right side baseboards over the ends of the front and rear baseboards. Align the top of the boards and keep the outside edges of the front and rear baseboards flush with the ends of the side boards, then fasten them together using 16d box nails.

2. Measure 49½" from the outside edge of the rear baseboard and mark the side baseboards. Place the middle baseboard in front of the marks, then attach it using 16d nails. **Note:** The middle baseboard is not placed in the exact middle of the base.

3. Set a post in the appropriate corner. Plumb adjacent sides of the post, then drive 16d nails through the baseboards to fasten the post in place. Do this for each post. The two 107" posts go in the front corners. The 139½" posts sit in the rear corners and on the rear side of the middle baseboard.

4. Measure from the bottom of the middle posts and mark the rear of the posts at 11¼" and 65". Place a 2 × 4 cross brace across the middle posts, aligning the bottom of the brace with the outside of the post at the 11¼" mark and the top of the brace at the outside of the opposite post at the 65" mark. Draw a line on the brace along the edge of the posts, then cut the brace using a circular saw. Repeat this step to measure and cut the second cross brace.

5. Attach the brace to the posts using 16d nails. Nail a 2 × 4 spacer to the posts at the locations of the second brace, then nail the brace to the spacers.

Step B: Frame the Clubhouse Floor

1. Measure from the bottom of the 139½" posts and mark the inside faces at 89". Install a double joist hanger on the face of each post so the bottom of the hanger is at the mark. Nail the hangers in place using 10d joist hanger nails.

2. Place two rim joists in each bracket, crowned side up, and nail them in place using 10d nails. Facenail the pairs of rim joists together using 16d box nails driven at a slight angle.

3. Mark the two joist locations on the front and rear rim joists. One joist is 24" on-center from the outside of the right side rim joist, the other is 24" on-center from the outside of the left side rim joist. Fasten the single joist hangers in place, then set the joists in the hangers, crowned side up. Nail the joists using 10d nails.

4. Measure from the outside of the rear rim joist and mark both joists at 13½" and 37". Place a trap-door header in front of each mark and endnail each through the joists using 16d nails.

A. *Nail the base together, then set the posts in the corners, making sure they are plumb before nailing them in place.*

BASE FRAMING

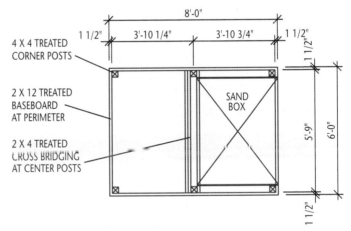

- 4 X 4 TREATED CORNER POSTS
- 2 X 12 TREATED BASEBOARD AT PERIMETER
- 2 X 4 TREATED CROSS BRIDGING AT CENTER POSTS

8'-0"
1 1/2" 3'-10 1/4" 3'-10 3/4" 1 1/2"
1 1/2" 5'-9" 6'-0" 1 1/2"

SAND BOX

FLOOR FRAMING CLUBHOUSE

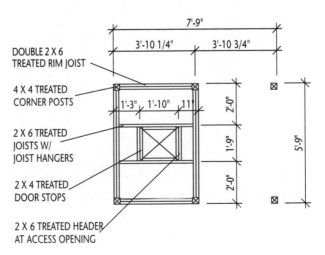

- DOUBLE 2 X 6 TREATED RIM JOIST
- 4 X 4 TREATED CORNER POSTS
- 2 X 6 TREATED JOISTS W/ JOIST HANGERS
- 2 X 4 TREATED DOOR STOPS
- 2 X 6 TREATED HEADER AT ACCESS OPENING

7'-9"
3'-10 1/4" 3'-10 3/4"
1'-3" 1'-10" 11"
2'-0" 1'-9" 2'-0" 5'-9"

B. *Fasten the joists in the joist hangers, then frame the access opening for the trapdoor.*

C. *Install decking over the joists. Cut out the access opening as the boards are fastened into place.*

D. *Build the trapdoor with the decking cut out of the access opening, then attach it to the deck with a hinge.*

Step C: Install the Floor Decking

1. Cut the first piece of decking at 69" using a circular saw, then cut 3½ × 3½" notches on both ends to fit around the posts using a jig saw. Place the board on the deck, flush with the outer rim joist. Drill two ³⁄₃₂" pilot holes in each end of the board and use 2½" wood screws to fasten it in place. Drill pilot holes and insert screws along the outer rims and joists.

2. Position the remaining boards so they overhang the rim joists. Space the boards about ⅛" apart. Drill pilot holes in the ends of the boards where they cross the outer rim joists. Fasten the decking with two screws per joist. As the trapdoor access opening is covered, cut each board flush with the header and joists, using a jig saw. (Save the waste for the trap door.)

3. Cut the last deck board to size and notch the ends to fit around the posts.

4. Snap a chalk line across the boards to mark the outside edge of the deck. Cut the boards at the mark using a circular saw. Use a jig saw for boards the circular saw cannot reach.

Step D: Build & Install the Trapdoor

1. Use the deck boards that were cut out of the access opening in the last step to build the trapdoor. Place the boards perpendicular to the 2 × 4 trapdoor nailers, overhanging the nailers 1½" on both ends and 2½" on both sides (keep in mind the door opens from the left side.) Drill pilot holes and attach the boards to the nailers using wood screws.

2. Make a mark in the center of the left side of the trapdoor 3" from the edge. Drill a 1" hole at the mark. Use a jig saw to cut from the outside edges of the hole to the edge of the trapdoor.

3. Facenail 2 × 4 trapdoor stops around the access opening, flush with the top of the headers and the

TRAPDOOR OPENING

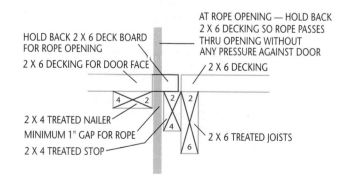

joists (the door stops sit below the deck boards).

4. Place the door in the access opening so the rope hole faces the left side of the clubhouse. Fasten a piano hinge to the right side of the trapdoor and to the deck boards to fasten the door in place.

Step E: Frame the Walls

1. Facenail the 43½" corner studs against the front and rear clubhouse posts using 16d nails.

2. Fasten a 62" top plate over the corner studs using 16d nails. Nail a 48" top plate over the right and left side posts. Nail a 69" top plate over the front and rear posts, then nail a 41" top plate over each 48" top plate to form a double top plate.

3. On the front of the clubhouse deck, measure 22½" from the outside of each corner and make a mark for the door opening. Toenail a door jamb outside of each mark, flush with the edge of the deck, using 16d nails. Use a level to make sure each jamb is plumb, then toenail them to the top plate.

4. Measure 30½" from the bottom of the door jambs and make a mark. Place the 24" door purlin above the marks and endnail through the jambs using 16d nails. Facenail a second door jamb against the standing jambs, driving 16d nails at a slight angle so they don't come through the other side.

5. Measure 22½" up from the deck and make a mark on the outside door jambs and corner studs. Nail 14½" purlins so the top of the purlin is flush with the marks.

6. Measure up from the deck and make a mark at 21" and 30½" on the corner studs at the rear of clubhouse and the left and right side corner posts. Install purlins above the marks. Mark each purlin 14" from the outside of the corner posts and install an 8" opening jamb outside of each mark using 16d nails.

E. *Install the purlins and jambs to all four sides of the clubhouse for the window and door openings.*

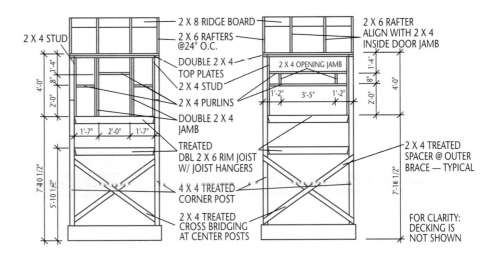

FRONT FRAMING

2 X 4 STUD

4'-0"
1'-4"
8"
2'-0"
7'-10 1/2"
5'-10 1/2"

1'-7" 2'-0" 1'-7"

2 X 8 RIDGE BOARD
2 X 6 RAFTERS @24" O.C.
DOUBLE 2 X 4 TOP PLATES
2 X 4 STUD
2 X 4 PURLINS
DOUBLE 2 X 4 JAMB
TREATED DBL 2 X 6 RIM JOIST W/ JOIST HANGERS
4 X 4 TREATED CORNER POST
2 X 4 TREATED CROSS BRIDGING AT CENTER POSTS

REAR FRAMING

2 X 4 OPENING JAMB

1'-2" 3'-5" 1'-2"

1'-4"
8"
2'-0"
4'-0"
7'-10 1/2"

2 X 6 RAFTER ALIGN WITH 2 X 4 INSIDE DOOR JAMB

2 X 4 TREATED SPACER @ OUTER BRACE — TYPICAL

FOR CLARITY: DECKING IS NOT SHOWN

RIGHT SIDE FRAMING

2 X 4 GABLE STUD

12
12

4'-0"
1'-4"
8"
2'-0"
3'-01/2"
5'-10 1/2"

1'-2" 1'-8" 1'-2"

2 X 8 RIDGE BOARD
2 X 6 RAFTERS @ 24" O.C.
DOUBLE 2 X 4 TOP PLATES
2 X 4 PURLINS
2 X 4 OPENING JAMB
DBL 2 X 6 RIM JOIST W/ JOIST HANGERS
4 X 4 TREATED CORNER POST
2 X 12 TREATED BASEBOARD

LEFT SIDE FRAMING

2 X 4 GABLE STUD

4'-0"
1'-4"
8"
2'-0"
3'-01/2"
7'-10 1/2"
5'-10 1/2"

1'-2" 1'-8" 1'-2"

2 X 4 PURLINS
2 X 4 OPENING JAMB

RAFTER SECTION

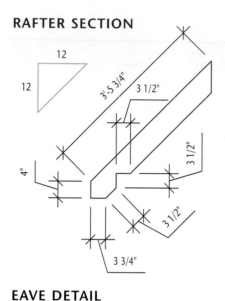

12
12

3'-5 3/4"
3 1/2"
3 1/2"
4"
3 1/2"
3 3/4"

EAVE DETAIL

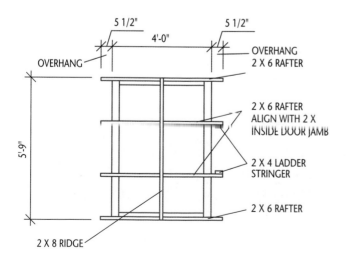

PLYWOOD ROOF SHEATHING

ASPHALT SHINGLES OVER 15 LB FELT

CONTINUOUS METAL ROOF EDGE

1 X 6 FASCIA BOARD

1 X 6 T&G V-JT BOARDS EXTEND UP TO TOP OF WALL NOTCH AROUND RAFTER TAILS

2 X 6 RAFTERS

HOLD DOWN CLIP EACH RAFTER

2 X 4

DOUBLE 2 X 4 TOP PLATES

2 X 4 WOOD STUD

5 1/2"

CLUBHOUSE ROOF FRAMING

5 1/2"
5 1/2"
4'-0"
OVERHANG
OVERHANG
2 X 6 RAFTER
5'-9"

2 X 6 RAFTER ALIGN WITH 2 X INSIDE DOOR JAMB

2 X 4 LADDER STRINGER

2 X 6 RAFTER

2 X 8 RIDGE

Step F: Frame the Roof

1. Cut two 2 × 6 pattern rafters following the Rafter Section illustration. Use a jig saw to cut the bird's mouth. Place the rafters on the top plates and test fit them using a 2 × 8 spacer block. Cut the remaining six rafters.

2. Mark the rafter locations on the top plates and the ridge board. The end rafters sit flush with the outside edge of the top plates on the right and left sides. Align the middle rafters with the inside door jambs, 22½" from the outside edge of the right and left top plates and ridge board.

3. Toenail the rafters to the top plates using 16d nails. Align the top of the rafters with the top of the ridge board and nail the rafters using 16d nails. Reinforce each rafter connection by fastening a hold down clip to the outside of the plates and the side of the rafter using 6d nails.

4. Measure the distance from the bottom of the ridge board to the top plate on the left and right sides. Cut a 2 × 4 support to that measurement for each side and install the supports between the top plates and the ridge board. Toenail the supports using 16d nails.

F. *Nail the rafters to the top plates and the ridge board at the proper locations. Install clips to reinforce the connection between the rafters and the top plates.*

Step G: Shingle the Roof

1. Fasten a fascia board to the ends of the rafters on each side using 6d galvanized finish nails. Align the top of the fascia with the top of the rafter.

2. Install ½" plywood sheathing on the rafters. Use 6d box nails driven approximately every 6" along the edges and 12" in the field to fasten the sheathing to the rafters.

3. Place metal roof edge (drip edge) along the sides and bottom of the sheathing. Cut a 45° miter on the ends using metal snips. Keep the ends flush with the ends of the fascia, and install using galvanized roofing nails. Overlap joints in the roof edge by 2".

4. Cover the roof with 15# felt paper and staple it to the sheathing. The paper should cover the roof edge. Work from the bottom edge to the peak, overlapping the lower row of paper by 2".

5. Snap a chalk line 11½" from the front of the roof edge. Cut 6" off the end of a shingle and position it upside down on the roof so the bottom is flush with the chalk line and the side overhangs the drip edge by ⅜". Fasten the shingle using galvanized roofing nails. Install the remaining shingles in the starter row.

6. Install the first row of shingles right side up, aligning the shingles with the bottom and side of the starter row. For the second row, overhang the first shingle on the end by half a tab. Move each new row over half a tab. Overlap the shingles just above the tab slots. Measure down from the ridge every few rows to make sure the rows are straight. Snap a chalk line ⅜" past the roof edge along the sides of the roof and cut the overhanging shingles along the line.

7. Cut ridge caps from shingles using a utility knife. Snap a chalk line 6" from the ridge and nail the ridge caps along the line. Cover any exposed roofing nails with roofing cement.

Step H: Install the Siding

1. Starting at a corner, align the edge of the siding with the outside edge of the corner post. Fasten the siding to the framing using 4d coated common nails. Drive two nails at the top and bottom of the board and at the purlins.

2. Install the next board, fitting the tongue-and-groove joint together and nailing it in place. Install the remaining boards the same way. Check every third board with a level to make sure it's plumb.

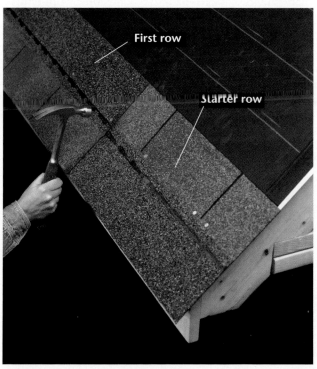

G. *Place the starter row of shingles upside down, then lay the first row of shingles over the top of it.*

H. *Nail the siding to the clubhouse, fitting it together at the tongue-and-groove joints. Cut the boards at the purlins and jambs for the openings.*

I. *Fasten the deck boards to the joists using deck screws. Leave ⅛" gap between the boards.*

DECK FLOOR FRAMING

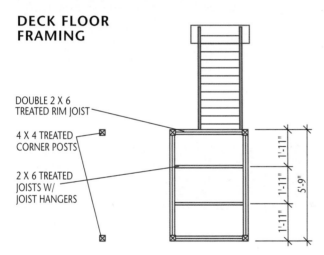

DOUBLE 2 X 6
TREATED RIM JOIST

4 X 4 TREATED
CORNER POSTS

2 X 6 TREATED
JOISTS W/
JOIST HANGERS

1'-11"
1'-11"
1'-11"
5'-9"

FLOOR PLAN

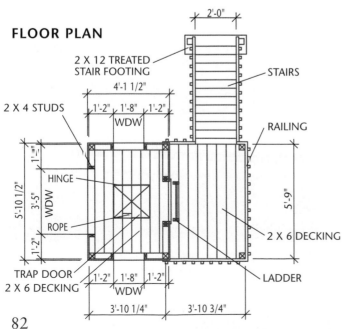

2 X 12 TREATED
STAIR FOOTING

STAIRS

2'-0"

4'-1 1/2"

1'-2" 1'-8" 1'-2"
WDW

2 X 4 STUDS

RAILING

1'-'"
HINGE
WDW
3'-5"
ROPE
5'-10 1/2"
1'-2"
5'-9"

2 X 6 DECKING

TRAP DOOR
2 X 6 DECKING

1'-2" 1'-8" 1'-2"
WDW

3'-10 1/4"   3'-10 3/4"

LADDER

Make the necessary adjustments in small increments. Overlap the boards at the corners.

3. On the front and rear sides of the clubhouse, cut notches in the top of the boards using a jig saw to fit around the rafters.

4. As the siding is installed, cut the boards at the purlins and jambs for the window openings.

5. Keep the siding at least 12" below the bottom of the purlin on the front door. Measure down 12" from the bottom of the purlin and 12" from the inside of a door jamb and make a mark. At the mark, draw a 12" radius on the siding, then cut along the mark using a jig saw to form the arched opening.

6. Nail the 2 × 8 door sill to the rim joist under the door opening. Align the top of the sill with the top of the decking

Step I: Build the Deck

1. Measure 65" from the bottom of the front and middle posts and make a mark. Install joist hangers on the inside faces of the posts. Align the bottoms of the hangers with the 65" marks. Place double rim joists in the hangers and nail them in place. Facenail the pairs of rim joists together.

2. Measure along the front and rear rim joists and mark the joist locations at 23" on-center from either side. Attach the single joist hangers and place the joists in the hangers.

3. Install the deck boards following the instructions in Step C.

4. Fasten the deck fascia boards to the deck using 2½" wood screws. Align the top of the fascia with the top of the deck boards. The front and back fascia are flush with the outside of the posts. The side fascia overlap the ends of the front and rear fascia.

STRINGER LAYOUT

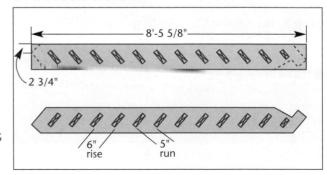

8'-5 5/8"

2 3/4"

6"
rise

5"
run

Stringer Layout: *Lay out the stair stringers using a framing square with tape at the proper locations following these measurements.*

Step J: Build the Stairs

1. Lay out the stair stringers on 2×10 pressure-treated lumber. Use tape to mark the rise measurement on one leg of a framing square. Tape the run measurement on the other leg. Beginning at one end of the stringer, place the square so the tape marks are flush with the edge of the board.

2. Outline the rise and run for the 12 treads following the Stringer Layout illustration. Draw in the tread outline on the bottom of each run line. Cut the stringer ends using a circular saw. Cut the notch in the end of the stringers to fit over the deck.

3. Place tread clips on the stringers, aligning them with the tread outlines. Drill ⅛" pilot holes through the holes in the clips, then fasten them using ¼ × 1¼" lag screws.

4. Attach angle brackets to the upper end of the stringers at the notch where they will butt against the deck fascia. Fasten the brackets using 4d joist hanger nails.

5. Center the stair footing under the stringers and fasten it using 2½" wood screws. The footing sits below the ground.

6. On the right side of the deck, measure from the front end of the fascia board and make a mark at 5" and 30½" for the stair stringers. Place the stringers on the rear side of the marks and fasten them to the deck by driving 4d joist hanger nails through the angle brackets into the fascia.

7. Starting at the top of the stringers, place the 2×6 treads on the tread clips. The starter tread is flush with the top of the deck and butted against the fascia. Align the front of the other treads with the tread outline on the stringers. Drill ³⁄₃₂" pilot holes in the bottom of the treads at the nail locations in the clips. Attach the treads using 1¼" galvanized lag screws. For the last tread, mark the hole locations with a pencil, remove the tread to drill the pilot holes, then replace it on the cleat and install the screws.

Step K: Install the Deck Railing

1. Place the two 42¼" deck rail posts on top of the stair footing, ½" from the end of each stringer. Use a level to plumb the posts, then clamp them to the stringers.

2. Drill two ⅜" holes at the bottom of the posts, spacing the holes about 4" apart and drilling all the way through the stringers. Counterbore each hole ½" deep using a 1" spade bit. Insert a ⅜ × 5" carriage bolt with washer through each hole. Place a washer and nut on each bolt and tighten them using a ratchet wrench.

J. *Place the stringers on the deck, then attach them by driving nails through the angle brackets.*

HEAD OF STAIR

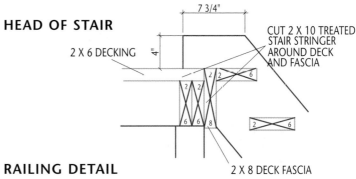

7 3/4"
2 X 6 DECKING
4"
CUT 2 X 10 TREATED STAIR STRINGER AROUND DECK AND FASCIA
2 X 8 DECK FASCIA

RAILING DETAIL

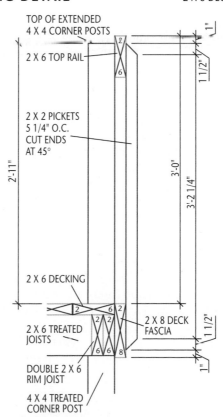

TOP OF EXTENDED 4 X 4 CORNER POSTS
2 X 6 TOP RAIL
1"
1 1/2"
2 X 2 PICKETS 5 1/4" O.C. CUT ENDS AT 45°
2'-11"
3'-0"
3'-2 1/4"
2 X 6 DECKING
2 X 6 TREATED JOISTS
2 X 8 DECK FASCIA
1 1/2"
DOUBLE 2 X 6 RIM JOIST
1"
4 X 4 TREATED CORNER POST

K. *Trace the location of the side rails onto the clubhouse siding, cut the siding away, then fasten the rail in place.*

L. *Use a spacer block for equal spacing between balusters (inset). Fasten each baluster to the fascia and rail using wood screws.*

3. Place the 41¼" post in the corner where the inside stringer butts against the deck fascia. Keep the post 1" above the bottom of the fascia. Drill two ⅜" holes through the post and stringer, counterbore ½" deep holes, and attach the post using carriage bolts.

4. Measure from the top of the deck and make a mark on the outside edge of the middle and front corner posts at 30½". Place the 69" deck rail across the front corner posts so the bottom of the rail is at the 30½" mark and the ends are flush with the outside edges of the posts. Drill ³⁄₃₂" pilot holes in the rail and fasten it to the posts using 2½" wood screws.

5. Place the 50" rails along the left and right sides of the deck, overlapping the ends of the front rail. Drill pilot holes, then insert a single wood screw into one of the holes, but don't tighten it. Level the rail and trace where the end of the rail overlaps the siding on the clubhouse. Lower the rail and carefully cut the tongue-and-groove siding at the mark to expose the middle post. Replace the rail and secure it to the posts using wood screws. Do the same with the rail on the other side.

Step L: Install the Balusters

1. Drill two ⅛" pilot holes near the bottom end of each baluster (picket), spaced about 4" apart. Drill two pilot holes near the top of the balusters, spaced 1½" apart. For the rear balusters, drill the top holes ¾" apart.

2. Fasten the 2 × 2 baluster nailer to the rear of the middle posts, butted against the bottom of the

clubhouse, using wood screws.

3. Measure 1" from the top of the deck rails and make a mark on each end. Snap a chalk line across the marks.

4. Cut a 2 × 6 spacer block at 3¾". Place the first baluster at a corner with the top edge flush with the chalk line, make sure the baluster is plumb, then fasten it to the rail and fascia using 2½" wood screws. Install the remaining balusters using the spacer block to ensure equal spacing between each baluster. Keep the balusters tight against the spacer, flush with the chalk line. Check every third or forth baluster with a level to make sure it's plumb. Make any necessary adjustments in small increments.

5. Install the balusters at the rear of the deck flush with the top of the 2 × 2 nailer.

Step M: Install Railing & Balusters on the Stairs

1. Cut the rail on the right side of the deck flush with the side of the posts at the top of the stairs, using a reciprocating saw.

2. Install a baluster at the top end of both stringers, 1" from the bottom edge of the stringer. Clamp a 2 × 6 top rail onto the post at the bottom of the stairs, keeping the rail 1" above the top of the post. Making sure the rail is 1" above the baluster, clamp the other end of the rail to the post at the top of the stairs. Trace the top and inside edges of this post onto the rail. The top of the rail will need to be cut back to be flush with the top of the post. Remove the rail and make the cuts using a jig saw.

3. Clamp the rail to the posts again. Drill pilot

M. *Fasten the top rail in place, then use a level to mark a plumb line from the end of the stringer to the rail. Cut the rail at the mark.*

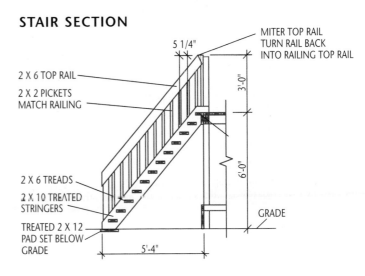

N. *Attach braces to the posts and along the baseboards, then install side plates over the braces.*

holes and fasten the rail into place using three wood screws per connection.

4. Place a level against the end of the stringer and draw a vertical line on the top rail that's plumb with the stringer. With the top rail in place, cut the vertical line using a reciprocating saw. Repeat steps 2 through 4 to install the opposite top rail.

5. Snap a chalk line from the top of the post at the bottom of the stairs to the top of the baluster at the top of the stairs.

6. Install balusters along the stairs, flush with the chalk line, using the 3¾" spacer to keep an equal distance between them.

Step N: Install Side Plates for the Sandbox

1. Measure 1½" from the bottom edge of each sandbox brace and cut a 45° angle using a miter saw.

2. Place a brace on the rear side of both front corner posts so the top of the brace is flush with the top of the 2 × 12 base boards. Drill two pilot holes in each brace, then attach them to the posts using wood screws.

3. Measure 21" from the front side of the middle posts and mark the baseboards. Attach a brace at the marks, flush with the top of the baseboards. Drill pilot holes through the baseboards, then install wood screws to secure the braces.

4. Place the side plates between the front and middle posts. Align the outside edge with the outside edge of the baseboard. Fasten the side plates to the baseboards and the braces using wood screws.

STAIR SECTION

5 1/4"

MITER TOP RAIL
TURN RAIL BACK
INTO RAILING TOP RAIL

2 X 6 TOP RAIL

2 X 2 PICKETS
MATCH RAILING

3'-0"

2 X 6 TREADS

2 X 10 TREATED
STRINGERS

6'-0"

TREATED 2 X 12
PAD SET BELOW
GRADE

GRADE

5'-4"

SANDBOX PLAN

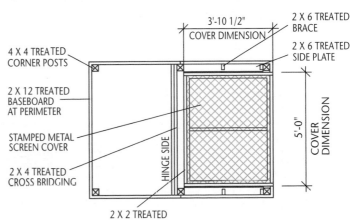

3'-10 1/2"
COVER DIMENSION

2 X 6 TREATED
BRACE

2 X 6 TREATED
SIDE PLATE

4 X 4 TREATED
CORNER POSTS

2 X 12 TREATED
BASEBOARD
AT PERIMETER

STAMPED METAL
SCREEN COVER

2 X 4 TREATED
CROSS BRIDGING

HINGE SIDE

5'-0"
COVER DIMENSION

2 X 2 TREATED

O. *Raise the sandbox cover and mark the locations for the latches on the cross braces.*

P. *Use a level to make sure the ladder is plumb, then attach it to the rafter tails above the door opening and to the deck floor.*

Step O: Build & Attach Sandbox Cover (Optional)

1. Place the 57" sandbox cover frames inside the edges of the 46½" frames. Drill pilot holes and fasten the frame together using wood screws.

2. Center 2 × 2 stops on the inside edge of the frame using wood screws. Install a stop through the center of the cover for additional support. Place the screen over the stops and staple it into place. To cover the sharp edges of the screen, cut screen moldings to size to fit over the screen, then nail it to the 2 × 2 stops using brad nails.

3. Place the cover over the sandbox so the front is flush with the front of the baseboard. Fasten two hinges to the rear of the sandbox cover and to the middle base plate. Fasten a handle at the center of the front of the cover.

4. Raise the sandbox cover and mark the locations where the top crosses the bracing for the center posts. Install a 2 × 4 spacer at the mark on the cross brace furthest away from the cover. Attach a gate latch on both cross braces at the marks and fasten a hook on both ends of the cover.

Step P: Build & Attach the Ladder

1. Measure from the bottom of the 68" ladder stringers and make a mark at 24", 16", and 8".

HINGE JAMB

4 X 4 TREATED POST
2 X 4 TREATED COVER FRAME
WIRE CLOTH SCREEN
HINGE
2 X 2 TREATED STOP
2 X 12 TREATED BASE
GRADE

LIFT JAMB

LIFT HANDLE
GRADE

SIDE JAMB

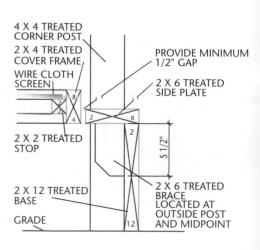

4 X 4 TREATED CORNER POST
2 X 4 TREATED COVER FRAME
WIRE CLOTH SCREEN
PROVIDE MINIMUM 1/2" GAP
2 X 6 TREATED SIDE PLATE
2 X 2 TREATED STOP
5 1/2"
2 X 12 TREATED BASE
2 X 6 TREATED BRACE LOCATED AT OUTSIDE POST AND MIDPOINT
GRADE

Q. *Insert the rope through the supports and ridge board, letting the other end pass freely through the opening in the trapdoor.*

Center the mark from front to back. Drill a ¾" hole at the marks ½" deep.

2. Insert the three 22" galvanized pipe rungs in the holes. Place the ladder ends inside the ends of the ladder stringers and fasten them together by drilling pilot holes and using wood screws.

3. Stand the ladder assembly upright and place it against the rafter tails just inside the fascia board. Make sure the ladder is plumb, then attach it to the rafters using wood screws.

4. Fasten the other end of the ladder to the deck by driving wood screws through the ladder end into the decking.

Step Q: Attach the Rope

1. Center the two 20" rope supports on either side of the ridge board over the trapdoor opening and attach them using 16d nails. Using a plumb bob hung from the ridge board, find the location on the ridge directly above the rope opening in the trapdoor. Mark the location on the ridge. Using a framing square, transfer the mark to the side of the rope support, then drill a 1" hole through the supports and ridge board.

2. Insert the rope through the hole and securely tie the end. Allow the other end to run through the rope opening. Make sure it does not apply any pressure against the trapdoor.

3. Tie knots in the rope every 12" to provide support to climbers.

LADDER AT EVE & AT DECK

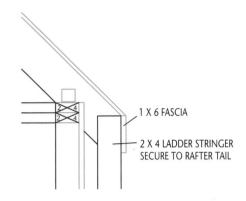

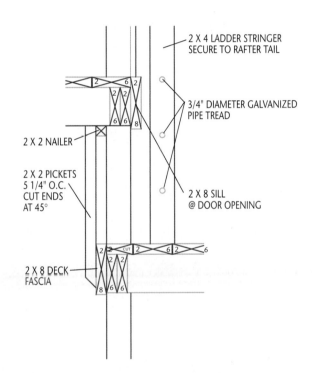

1 X 6 FASCIA

2 X 4 LADDER STRINGER SECURE TO RAFTER TAIL

2 X 4 LADDER STRINGER SECURE TO RAFTER TAIL

3/4" DIAMETER GALVANIZED PIPE TREAD

2 X 2 NAILER

2 X 2 PICKETS 5 1/4" O.C. CUT ENDS AT 45°

2 X 8 SILL @ DOOR OPENING

2 X 8 DECK FASCIA

ROPE SUPPORT

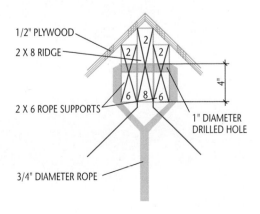

1/2" PLYWOOD

2 X 8 RIDGE

2 X 6 ROPE SUPPORTS

1" DIAMETER DRILLED HOLE

3/4" DIAMETER ROPE

Tree House

No other structure lends itself to outdoor play quite like a tree house. There's something magical about playing in a tree. There's also the added thrill of being able to play in a miniature house above the ground.

Tree houses come in all shapes, sizes, models, and designs, some more professional looking than others. While tree houses should be fun, they also need to be safe. The tree house featured here is both. The front half is open at the top to allow children to look out at their surroundings. The support system holds the tree house securely in place, the railing prevents falls, and the ladder ensures a safe entrance and exit. The roof is constructed with fiberglass panels that allow light to enter.

While almost any full-size tree will serve as a host for the tree house, there are a few important precautions to take. Make sure the tree has a strong base of at least 12" in diameter. It must be alive and healthy. If the leaves on the tree are brown and starting to wither, and it's not autumn yet, the tree could have a disease and should not be used. Choose a tree that doesn't produce a lot of sap so your children will not get covered in it. Caution your kids not to peel bark off the tree or it will eventually kill the tree.

This project calls for the tree house to sit six feet off the ground. You can adjust this height to suit your particular tree, but be careful not to place the structure too low or the diagonal braces will run into the ground before touching the tree. The diagonal braces are tricky to cut. Nevertheless, it's important they are done correctly and properly fastened to the tree house and the tree.

MATERIAL LIST

DESCRIPTION	QTY./SIZE	MATERIAL
Support System		
Timber diagonal support	4 @ 8'-0"	4 × 6 treated timber
Spikes	8 @ 12"	Timber to tree (2 per timber)
Adjustable angles	8	Simpson LS50
Floor Framing		
Rim joists	7 @ 8'-0"	2 × 8 treated
Rim joist	1 @ 10'-0"	2 × 8 treated
Joists and joist supports	8 @ 8'-0"	2 × 8 treated
Joist hangers	4 with nails	Simpson U26
Beam hangers	4 with nails	Simpson U26-2
Spikes	6 @ 8"	Support to tree (3 per support)
Spikes	6 @ 8"	Joists to tree (3 per joist)
Decking	17 @ 8'-0"	2 × 6 treated
Wall Framing		
Girts/studs/top plates	8 @ 8'-0"	2 × 4 SPF construction grade no.2
Posts	9 @ 6'-0"	4 × 4 treated
Metal connectors	9 with nails	Posts to joist rims – Simpson 00L
Metal connectors	9 with nails	Posts to roof timbers – Simpson 88L
Roof Framing		
Timber beams	4 @ 8'-0"	4 × 6 treated
Rafters	2 @ 8'-0"	2 × 6 SPF construction grade no. 2
Metal connectors	8 with nails	Beam to beam – Simpson A34

DESCRIPTION	QTY./SIZE	MATERIAL
Roof Framing (cont.)		
Spikes	6 @ 8"	Rafters to tree (3 per rafter)
Roofing panels	5 @ 2'-0" × 10'-0"	Corrugated fiberglass panels
Closure strips	4 @ 9'-0"	wood strips
Ladder		
Stringer	2 @ 10'-0"	2 × 8 treated
Rungs	3 @ 8'-0"	2 × 6 treated
Ladder footing	1 @ 4'-0"	2 × 12 treated
Tread clip	18	1½" × 1½" × 5" 16-gauge angle
Galvanized wood screws	120 @ 1¼"	Angle to treads
Exterior Finishes		
Siding	40 @ 8'-0"	1 × 6 T&G V-JT cedar boards
Pickets	15 @ 8'-0"	1 × 6 S4S cedar
Galvanized wood screws	120 @ 1¼"	Pickets
Railing		
Top rail	2 @ 9'-0"	2 × 6 S4S cedar
Galvanized wood screws	75 @ 1½"	Railing
Miscellaneous		
Galvanized box nails	16d – 3 pounds	Lumber to lumber
Box nails	8d – 2 pounds	Lumber to lumber
Finish nails	6d	Closure strips to rafters
Galvanized finish nails	6d – 1½ pound	Siding
Galvanized hex-headed panel screws	96 @ 1¼"	Panels to closure strips
Galvanized wood screws	210 @ 2½"	Decking

Note: When working with treated lumber, hot-dipped galvanized or stainless steel nails, fasteners, and fittings are recommended.

HOW TO BUILD A TREE HOUSE

Step A: Install the Joist Supports

1. Measure 63¼" from the bottom of the tree and make a mark. **Note:** this measurement is for a deck height of 72" from the ground. If you want a different deck height, adjust as necessary.

2. Cut a 2 × 8 joist support at 96", using a circular saw. Place the top edge of the support flush with the mark on the tree, centering the support with the middle of the tree. Drive an 8" spike through the support into the tree, but don't nail it tight. Place a level on the top edge of the support, level it, then finish driving the spike. Nail two more spikes through the support.

3. Use a level to mark the location of the second support on the opposite side of the tree. Tack the 120" rim joist support in place at the mark, level it, then fasten it to the tree using three 8" spikes. The ends of this support should run past the ends of the first support.

4. Place a large framing square at the end of the first support and mark the end on the second support. Do this on each end, then cut the second support at the marks using a circular saw.

Step B: Build the Floor Frame

1. Cut eight 2 × 8 joists at 90". Place one joist on each side of the tree, perpendicular to the supports. Use a carpenter's square to square the joists with the supports and each other. Center the joists over the supports, then tack them to the tree using 16d nails.

2. Place a second joist against each joist on the

tree, flush on the top and ends, and drive three 8" spikes through the second joist, through the first joist, and into the tree. Facenail the sets of joists together using 16d box nails driven at a slight angle so they don't come out the other side.

3. Center a joist over the supports so the outside edge of the joist is 1½" from the ends of the supports. Toenail the joist to the supports using 8d box nails. Do this on the front and back sides.

4. Cut two rim joists at 93" and place them over the ends of the joists installed in the last step. Keep the joists flush at the top. Endnail the joists together using 16d nails. Install beam hangers on the rim joists where they intersect the joists on the tree. Fasten the hangers using joist hanger nails.

5. Measure the distance between the joists nailed to the tree and the joists at the ends of the supports. Mark the right and left side rim joists at the midpoints and install joist hangers over the marks using joist hanger nails. The nails will go through the joist, but will be covered by the outside rim joist.

6. Set joists in the hangers, then fasten them in place using 1½" joist hanger nails.

Note: Don't stand on the frame until the diagonal supports are installed.

Step C: Attach Diagonal Supports & Complete the Floor Frame

1. Cut a 45° angle on one end of the four 4 × 6 timber diagonal supports. Mark the angled ends following the Diagonal Support drawing, then carefully cut the angles and notches using a jig saw and miter saw.

2. Set a support under a corner of the floor fram-

FLOOR FRAMING PLAN

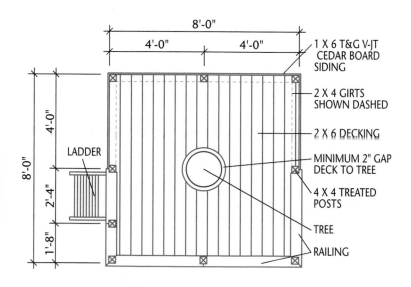

1 X 6 T&G V-JT CEDAR BOARD SIDING

2 X 4 GIRTS SHOWN DASHED

2 X 6 DECKING

MINIMUM 2" GAP DECK TO TREE

4 X 4 TREATED POSTS

TREE

RAILING

LADDER

A. *Fasten the second support in place, level with the first one, then cut the ends flush with the first support.*

ing and mark the other end where it crosses the tree. Cut a 45° angle at the mark. **Note:** You may have to set the support in place, mark the end, and make the cut several times before finding a perfect fit. Be careful not to cut the brace too short. Fasten the support in place by driving 16d nails through the joists into the support and driving two 12" spikes through the support into the tree. Reinforce the connections by fastening LS50 adjustable angles to the support and tree, and to the support and rim joist using 8d nails. The angles adjust from 0° to 135°. You can bend the angle one time only. Do this for all four corners.

3. Cut two rim joists at 93" and place them on the outside of the front and rear joists. These rim joists sit on the edge of the 2 × 8 supports. Align the ends of the rim joists with the outside edges of the side rim joists. Facenail the rim joists to the front and back joists and endnail to the side rim joists using 16d nails.

4. Cut two more rim joists at 96" and facenail them to the side rim joists, overlapping the ends of the joists installed in the last step. Nail the corners together using 16d nails.

Step D: Install Corner Posts & Timber Beams

1. Cut two 4 × 4 back corner posts at 66" and two front corner posts at 54½" using a reciprocating saw.

2. Set a piece of plywood over the floor framing to stand on. Place the back posts in the rear corners and the front posts in the front corners, flush with the outside edges of the rim joists. Plumb the posts using a level, then toenail them to the joists using 16d nails. Reinforce the connections by fastening a Simpson 88L metal connector to each post and outer rim joist using 16d nails.

3. Cut two 4 × 6 timber beams at 96". Set one beam on the rear corner posts and the other beam on the front corner posts, flush with the outside edges of the posts. Toenail the beams in place, then fasten Simpson 88L metal connectors to the posts and the beams.

4. Nail 2 × 4 scrap lumber on the ends of the beams installed in the last step. Clamp a 4 × 6 side beam against the ends of the front and rear beams using the scrap lumber, making sure the ends of the

DIAGONAL SUPPORT

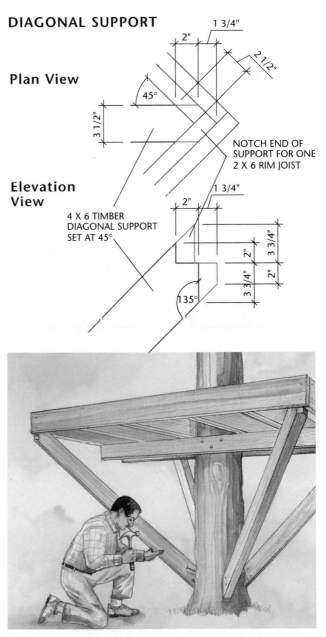

Plan View

1 3/4"
2"
2 1/2"
45°
3 1/2"

NOTCH END OF SUPPORT FOR ONE 2 X 6 RIM JOIST

Elevation View

1 3/4"
2"
3 3/4"
2"
3 3/4"
2"
3 3/4"
135°

4 X 6 TIMBER DIAGONAL SUPPORT SET AT 45°

B. *Mark the midpoints between the joists, install joist hangers, then set the joists in the hangers and nail them in place.*

C. *Notch one end of each support brace to fit under the rim joist. Fasten one end under a corner of the floor and the other end to the tree.*

LEFT SIDE FRAMING

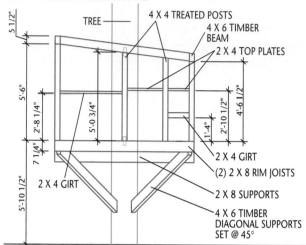

TREE
4 X 4 TREATED POSTS
4 X 6 TIMBER BEAM
2 X 4 TOP PLATES
5 1/2"
5'-6"
2'-8 1/4"
5'-0 3/4"
4'-6 1/2"
2'-10 1/2"
1'-4"
7 1/4"
5'-10 1/2"
2 X 4 GIRT
2 X 4 GIRT
(2) 2 X 8 RIM JOISTS
2 X 8 SUPPORTS
4 X 6 TIMBER DIAGONAL SUPPORTS SET @ 45°

RIGHT SIDE FRAMING

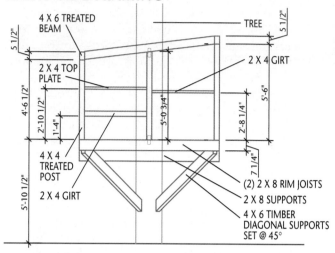

4 X 6 TREATED BEAM
2 X 4 TOP PLATE
4 X 4 TREATED POST
2 X 4 GIRT
TREE
2 X 4 GIRT
5 1/2"
4'-6 1/2"
2'-10 1/2"
1'-4"
5'-0 3/4"
5'-6"
2'-8 1/4"
7 1/4"
5'-10 1/2"
(2) 2 X 8 RIM JOISTS
2 X 8 SUPPORTS
4 X 6 TIMBER DIAGONAL SUPPORTS SET @ 45°

FRONT FRAMING

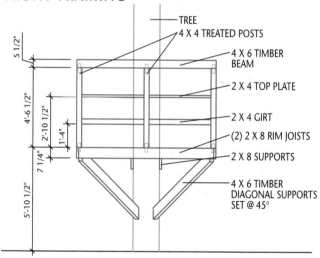

TREE
4 X 4 TREATED POSTS
4 X 6 TIMBER BEAM
2 X 4 TOP PLATE
2 X 4 GIRT
(2) 2 X 8 RIM JOISTS
2 X 8 SUPPORTS
4 X 6 TIMBER DIAGONAL SUPPORTS SET @ 45°
5 1/2"
4'-6 1/2"
2'-10 1/2"
1'-4"
7 1/4"
5'-10 1/2"

BACK FRAMING

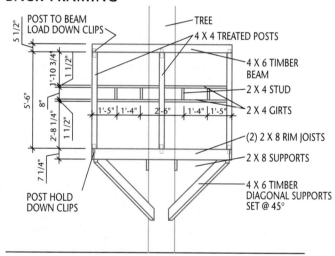

POST TO BEAM LOAD DOWN CLIPS
TREE
4 X 4 TREATED POSTS
4 X 6 TIMBER BEAM
2 X 4 STUD
2 X 4 GIRTS
(2) 2 X 8 RIM JOISTS
2 X 8 SUPPORTS
4 X 6 TIMBER DIAGONAL SUPPORTS SET @ 45°
POST HOLD DOWN CLIPS
5 1/2"
1'-10 3/4"
1 1/2"
5'-6"
8"
2'-8 1/4"
1 1/2"
7 1/4"
1'-5" 1'-4" 2'-6" 1'-4" 1'-5"

D. *Place a side beam between the front and back beams, mark the side beam, cut it to length, then fasten it in place using metal connectors.*

E. *Mark the middle posts where they cross the timber beams. Cut the posts at the marks, then fasten them in place using metal connectors.*

side beam extend past the inside edge of the two installed beams. Align the side beam with the top inside face of the front and rear beams, then draw a line along the inside edge of the front and rear beams onto the side beam. Do this on both front and rear sides.

5. Clamp a 2 × 6 rafter on the end of the beams and repeat the last step to draw a line onto the rafters along the inside edge of the beams. Cut the rafter at the marks using a circular saw, then use it as a template to mark and cut the second rafter. Place the rafters on either side of the tree, flush with the top of the timber beams. Toenail the rafters to the beams using 16d nails. Drive three 8" spikes through each rafter into the tree.

6. Cut the side beams at the marks using a reciprocating saw. Set the side beams in place between the front and back beams. Toenail the beams in place. Install Simpson A34 metal connectors on the inside corners of the beams using 8d × 1½" nails.

Step E: Attach the Middle Posts

1. Cut a 4 × 4 post at 54½". Mark the center point between the front corner posts and install the post over the mark. Align the outside of the post with the outside edges of the rim joist and the timber beam. Use a level to plumb the post, then toenail it in place. Secure the post to the rim joist and timber beam using Simpson 88L metal connectors.

2. Cut a post at 66" and install it at the center of the back side by repeating step 1.

3. Place a post at the center of the right side. Keep the bottom end on the rim joist, plumb the post

using a level, and mark along the top edge of the post where it crosses the timber beam. Cut the post at the mark, then toenail it to the rim joist and the timber beam. Secure the connections by installing metal connectors. Repeat this step for the left side.

4. On the left side, measure 24" from the front edge of the middle post and mark the rim joist. Set a post in front of the mark, then mark the top of the post where it crosses the timber beam. Cut the post at the mark, then install it at the mark on the rim joist using metal connectors.

Step F: Build the Floor

1. Use a jig saw to cut a 3½ × 3½" notch on each end of the first deck board to fit around the posts. Place the board on the right side of the tree house, aligning the ends with the outside edges of the rim joists, then mark the board at the middle post location. Cut a 3½ × 3½" notch at the mark.

2. Set the first deck board in place. Drill two ³⁄₃₂" pilot holes at both ends of the deck board, then fasten it to the rim joists using 2½" galvanized wood screws. Install two screws in the deck board where it crosses each joist and every 16" along the side.

3. Fasten the remaining boards to the frame. Since the boards are precut to 96", they should align with the outside edges of the front and back rim joists. Space the boards about ⅛" apart. Drill ³⁄₃₂" pilot holes in the ends of the boards where they cross the rim joists. Fasten each board using two screws per joist. If necessary, add blocking to support ends of boards that fall in line with middle posts.

4. Every three or four boards, measure the

F. *Install the decking, cutting the boards to fit around the tree and posts. Fasten the boards to the joists using galvanized wood screws.*

BUILDING SECTION

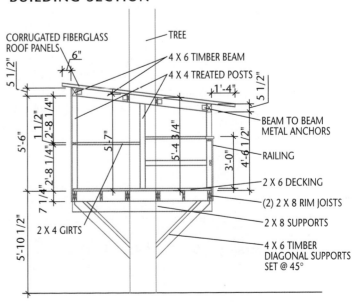

CORRUGATED FIBERGLASS ROOF PANELS

TREE

4 X 6 TIMBER BEAM

4 X 4 TREATED POSTS

BEAM TO BEAM METAL ANCHORS

RAILING

2 X 6 DECKING

(2) 2 X 8 RIM JOISTS

2 X 8 SUPPORTS

4 X 6 TIMBER DIAGONAL SUPPORTS SET @ 45°

2 X 4 GIRTS

93

FLOOR PLAN

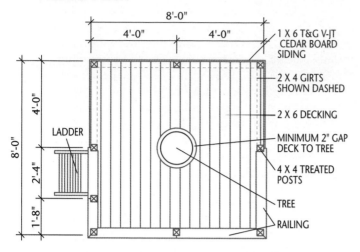

distance to the outside edge of the left side rim joist. Take a measurement from both ends of the board to make sure they're equal. Make sure the distance to the edge will allow the last board to sit flush with the outside edge of the rim joist. If needed, make slight adjustments to the spacing between deck boards.

5. Measure and mark each board to fit around the tree. Keep the decking 2" away from the tree. Cut the boards at the marks using a jig saw then install them.

Step G: Lay Out the Stringers

1. Measure from the top of the deck and mark the posts on either side of the ladder opening at 18¾" and 34½".

2. Cut an 80° angle at the bottom of a 2 × 8 stringer using a circular saw. Set the stringer inside the ladder opening so the edge of the stringer butts against the deck and crosses the inside edge of the post at the 18¾" mark. Mark the stringer along the inside edge of the post and along the 34½" mark on the post.

3. Remove the stringer and cut it at the marks. Using the stringer as a template, place it over the second 2 × 8 stringer, make sure the edges are flush, trace the first stringer onto the second one, and cut along the marks.

4. Outline the rise and run locations for the rungs on the stringers following Illustration G. The ladder is assembled and installed in Step K.

Note: These measurements are for a 72" deck height. If your deck height is different, make the necessary adjustments to your stringers.

Step H: Install the Girts and Top Plates

1. Cut nine 2 × 4 girts and three 2 × 4 top plates at 42¾" using a circular saw.

2. On the front side of the tree house, measure

from the top of the deck boards and mark the posts at 14½" and 33". Set a girt on-edge above the 14½" marks on each side of the middle post. Align the outside edge of the girts with the outside edges of the posts, then toenail the girts in place with 8d nails.

3. Set a top plate flat above the 33" marks on both sides of the middle post. Align the outside edges of the plates and the posts, then toenail the plates in place.

4. On the back side, measure from the deck and mark the posts at 30¾" and 40¼". Position girts flat and toenail them to the posts above the marks, keeping the outside edges flush.

5. Cut four 2 × 4 studs at 8". Measure from the outside edge of the corner posts and mark the girts installed in the last step at 15½" and 33". Fasten the studs at the marks using 16d nails.

6. On the right side, mark the front and middle posts at 14½" and 33" above the deck. Toenail a girt on-edge above the 14½" marks on the front and middle posts. Toenail a top plate flat above the 33" marks on the posts. On the back and middle posts, make a mark 30¾" above the deck. Toenail a girt flat to the posts above the marks.

7. On the left side, mark the back and middle posts at 30¾" above the deck and install a girt flat above the marks.

8. Cut one 2 × 4 top plate at 24" and one at 15¼". Cut a 2 × 4 girt at 15¼". Mark the two middle rails and the front rail 14½" and 33" from the top of the deck. Install the 24" top plate flat between the two middle posts above the 33" marks. Install the 15¼" top plate flat between the middle and front corner posts at the same height. Install the girt on-edge above the 14½" marks.

Step I: Install the Siding

1. Starting in a back corner, place a 1 × 6 tongue-and-groove cedar board flush with the outside edge of the post and the bottom edge of the rim joist. Allow the top to extend past the timber beam. Nail the board at the top, bottom, and girt locations using 6d galvanized finish nails. Nail the board to the corner post every 16".

2. Install the next board, fitting together the tongue-and-groove joint. Install the remaining boards, checking every third board with a level to make sure it's plumb, and making any necessary adjustments in small increments. Install the siding on the back ends of the left and right sides of the tree house, overlapping the siding at the back corners. Rip the last board on the left and right sides to cover half of the middle posts.

3. Cut the siding flush with the top edge of the timber beams and cut out the window openings

LEFT SIDE ELEVATION

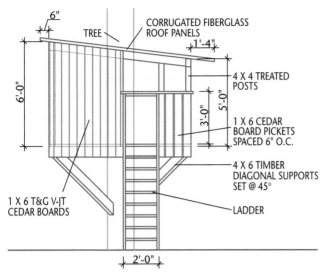

6"

TREE

CORRUGATED FIBERGLASS
ROOF PANELS

1'-4"

6'-0"

5'-0"

3'-0"

4 X 4 TREATED
POSTS

1 X 6 CEDAR
BOARD PICKETS
SPACED 6" O.C.

4 X 6 TIMBER
DIAGONAL SUPPORTS
SET @ 45°

1 X 6 T&G V-JT
CEDAR BOARDS

LADDER

2'-0"

RIGHT SIDE ELEVATION

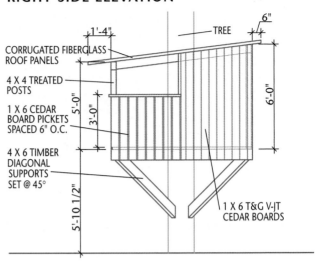

1'-4"

TREE

6"

CORRUGATED FIBERGLASS
ROOF PANELS

4 X 4 TREATED
POSTS

1 X 6 CEDAR
BOARD PICKETS
SPACED 6" O.C.

4 X 6 TIMBER
DIAGONAL
SUPPORTS
SET @ 45°

5'-0"

3'-0"

6'-0"

5'-10 1/2"

1 X 6 T&G V-JT
CEDAR BOARDS

FRONT ELEVATION

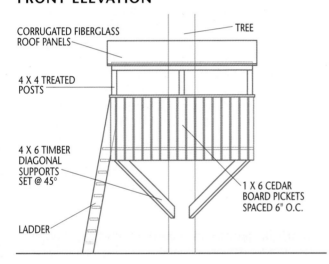

CORRUGATED FIBERGLASS
ROOF PANELS

TREE

4 X 4 TREATED
POSTS

4 X 6 TIMBER
DIAGONAL
SUPPORTS
SET @ 45°

LADDER

1 X 6 CEDAR
BOARD PICKETS
SPACED 6" O.C.

BACK ELEVATION

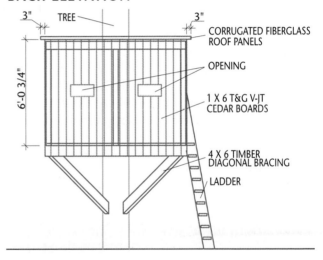

3"

TREE

3"

CORRUGATED FIBERGLASS
ROOF PANELS

OPENING

1 X 6 T&G V-JT
CEDAR BOARDS

4 X 6 TIMBER
DIAGONAL BRACING

LADDER

6'-0 3/4"

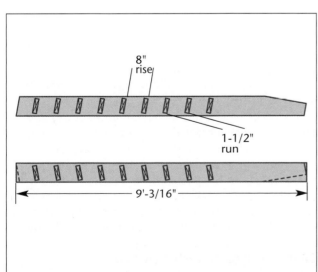

8"
rise

1-1/2"
run

9'-3/16"

G. *Cut the stringers and mark them with the rise and run locations for the ladder rungs.*

H. *Install the girts and top plates between the rails on all four sides of the tree house.*

I. *Butt the tongue-and-groove siding and the cedar board together at the middle post on the right side.*

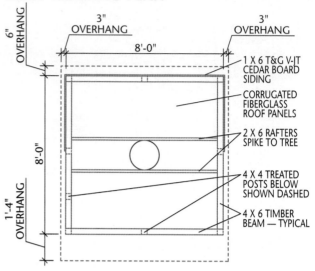

ROOF FRAMING PLAN

6" OVERHANG

3" OVERHANG

3" OVERHANG

8'-0"

8'-0"

1'-4" OVERHANG

1 X 6 T&G V-JT CEDAR BOARD SIDING

CORRUGATED FIBERGLASS ROOF PANELS

2 X 6 RAFTERS SPIKE TO TREE

4 X 4 TREATED POSTS BELOW SHOWN DASHED

4 X 6 TIMBER BEAM — TYPICAL

using a reciprocating saw.

4. Cut the 1 × 6 cedar picket boards for the front at 43¼" using a circular saw. Cut two boards from each piece of lumber. Align the first board with the outside edge of a front corner post and the bottom edge of the rim joist, drill ³⁄₃₂" pilot holes, then insert 1¼" wood screws. Install the remaining boards on the front and sides 6" on-center, giving ½" gap between boards.

5. Butt a cedar board against the tongue-and-grove siding on the right side middle post, and align the last board on the left side with the inside edge of the front ladder support.

Step J: Attach the Roof
1. Cut four closure strips at 98". Place the closure strips over the rafters and timber beams so they have a 1" overhang on each end. Attach the strips using 6d finish nails.

2. Place the first fiberglass roof panel over the closure strips so it overhangs the side by 3". The panel should overhang the back by approximately 6" and the front by 16", depending on how the panel sits in the closure strips. The panels are 120" long, so you have an extra two inches on the ends to work with. Attach the panel by drilling ⅛" holes through the peaks, not the troughs, and inserting 1¼" hex-headed panel screws with rubber gaskets at every fourth or fifth peak.

3. Set the next panel in place, overlapping the end by 3 to 4". Mark the panel where it crosses the tree. Cut out the mark, allowing a 3" gap for the tree, using a jig saw. Apply caulk to the last trough of the first panel, then set the second panel in place, drill pilot holes, and insert screws. Install the remaining panels the same way.

Step K: Build & Install the Ladder
1. Attach tread clips to the stringers, flush with the bottom of each rung outline. Drill ³⁄₃₂" pilot holes through the holes in the clips and fasten them to the stringers using 1¼" wood screws.

2. Cut nine 2 × 6 ladder rungs at 20½". This allows a ¼" gap on each end for the tread clips. Keep the outside edges of the stringers 24" apart and fasten the rungs to the clips using 1¼" wood screws.

3. Cut a 2 × 12 ladder footing at 36". Center the footing from back to front and side to side on the bottom of the ladder. Drill pilot holes into the footing, then fasten the footing to the stringers using 2½" wood screws.

4. Set the ladder in place with half of the footing below grade. Attach the ladder to the posts using 16d nails.

Step L: Attach the Top Rails
1. Cut two 2 × 6 top rails at 49½". Cut one end square and one end with a 45° angle, using a circular saw. Cut a top rail at 99" with a 45° angle on both ends.

2. Mark the ends of the rails following the Top Rail Corner and Top Rail @ Wall illustrations and cut the notches using a jig saw. Cut a notch in the left side top rail for the post at the top of the ladder.

3. Place the rails on the top plates, fitting the notches around the posts. Make sure the angles fit together tightly. Make any necessary cuts to get a tight fit, then secure the top rails in place by drilling pilot holes and inserting 2½" galvanized wood screws.

Step M: Celebrate with Your Kids!
Bring blankets and pillows and have a sleep out. Ghost stories are optional.

LADDER DETAIL

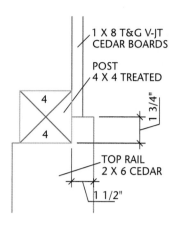

4 1/2"

1'-3 3/4"

2'-10 1/2"

GRADE TO TOP OF DECK DIMENSION

NAIL TO SIDE OF 4 X 4 POSTS

DECK LINE

ADJACENT STRUCTURE SHOWN DASHED

8" HEIGHT

2 X 6 TREATED LADDER RUNGS 1'-8 1/2" LONG

2 X 8 TREATED STRINGERS

2 X 12 TREATED LADDER FOOTING

GRADE

80°

TOP RAIL @ WALL

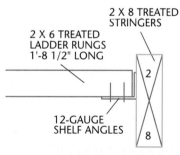

1 X 8 T&G V-JT CEDAR BOARDS

POST 4 X 4 TREATED

1 3/4"

TOP RAIL 2 X 6 CEDAR

1 1/2"

4

4

RAIL DETAIL

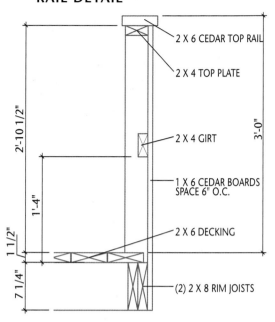

2 X 6 CEDAR TOP RAIL

2 X 4 TOP PLATE

2 X 4 GIRT

1 X 6 CEDAR BOARDS SPACE 6" O.C.

2 X 6 DECKING

(2) 2 X 8 RIM JOISTS

2'-10 1/2"

3'-0"

1'-4"

1 1/2"

7 1/4"

LADDER STRINGER

2 X 8 TREATED STRINGERS

2 X 6 TREATED LADDER RUNGS 1'-8 1/2" LONG

2

8

12-GAUGE SHELF ANGLES

TOP RAIL CORNER

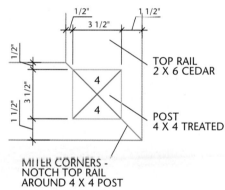

1/2"

3 1/2"

1 1/2"

1/2"

3 1/2"

1 1/2"

TOP RAIL 2 X 6 CEDAR

POST 4 X 4 TREATED

4

4

MITER CORNERS - NOTCH TOP RAIL AROUND 4 X 4 POST

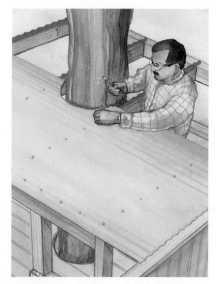

J. Cut the roof panel to fit around the tree, then set the panel in place over the first panel, drill pilot holes, and fasten the panel to the beams and rafters.

K. Assemble the ladder, then nail it to the insides of the posts.

L. Fit the top rails together at the angles so the posts fit inside the notches. Attach the rails to the top plates.

Tools & Materials

¼ × 4" galvanized eye bolts
with washers and nuts (3)
⅜ × .5" galvanized carriage bolts
with washers and nuts (12)
⅜ × 6" galvanized carriage bolts
with washers and nuts (4)
A-frame bracket (4)
Truss bracket w/screws (2)
⁵⁄₁₆ × 7" swing hanger unit (6)
10d galvanized nails
¼ × 2" lag screws
8d galvanized nails
Fence stakes (2)
Swings w/chairs (2)
Gym rings (1 set)
Climbing net
Leg anchors (6)
2 × 6 × 96"
cedar (2)
4 × 4 × 96"
cedar (6)
4 × 6 × 168"
cedar (1)

A-frame Swing Set with Climbing Wall

An A-frame swing set is a staple on playgrounds and in backyards. It's a structure we remember from our childhoods and one we want our kids to remember as they grow up. A-frame swing sets are popular because they're easy to build, appeal to kids of every age group, and look nice in the yard.

One of the benefits of A-frame swing sets is that you can choose from a variety of accessories to include on them. While this particular A-frame contains a climbing wall, swings, and gym rings, there are a host of other options available, such as trapeze bar, child's telescope, steering wheel, and gliders, just to name a few.

Just as there are a lot of accessories for A-frames, there are also a lot of gussets and brackets for building the structure. The ones suggested in this project are similar to most types of hardware on the market.

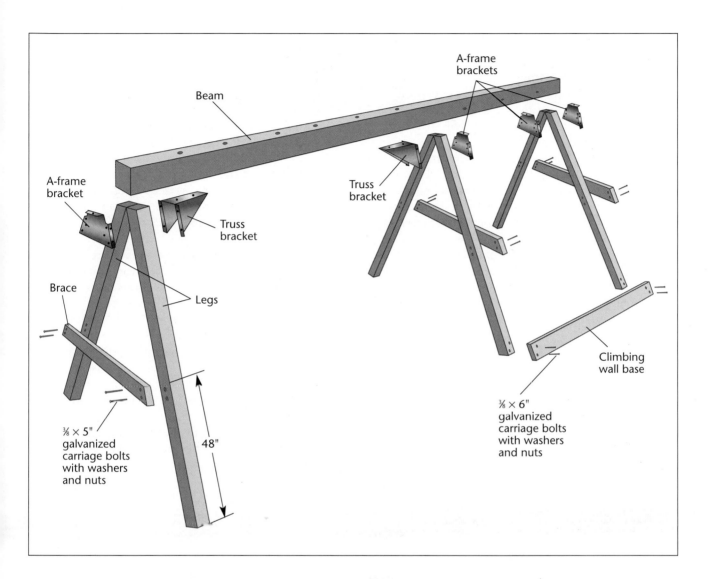

Beam

A-frame brackets

A-frame bracket

Truss bracket

Truss bracket

Brace

Legs

Climbing wall base

⅜ × 5" galvanized carriage bolts with washers and nuts

⅜ × 6" galvanized carriage bolts with washers and nuts

48"

CUTTING LIST

PART	QTY.	SIZE
Legs	6	4 × 4 × 96"
Beam	1	4 × 6 × 168"
Braces	3	2 × 6 cut to fit
Climbing wall base	1	2 × 6 × 54"

HOW TO BUILD AN A-FRAME SWING SET WITH CLIMBING WALL

Step A: Build the A-frames

1. Place a steel A-frame bracket at the top of a 4 × 4 leg so the inside of the leg is flush with the top of the bracket (the outside of the leg will stick out over the top of the bracket). Attach the bracket using 10d galvanized nails. Insert a second leg into the bracket and fasten it in place using 10d nails.

2. Turn the legs over and fasten a truss bracket at the top of the legs opposite the A-frame bracket using ¼ × 2" lag screws driven through pilot holes.

3. Turn the leg assembly over so the truss bracket is facing down. Measure 48" from the bottom of each leg and make a mark. Place a 2 × 6 brace across the legs with the top of the brace flush with the marks. Draw a line along each end of the brace where it crosses the outsides of the legs. Cut the brace at the lines using a circular saw.

4. Clamp the brace to the legs at the marks, flush with the outsides of the legs. Drill two ⅜" holes at each end of the brace, offsetting the holes. Drill all the way through the legs. Turn the frame over. Using the holes as a guide, drill ½"-deep recesses into the legs using a 1" spade bit. Insert ⅜ × 5" galvanized carriage bolts through the holes from the brace side. Place a washer and nut on the end of each bolt in

the recesses. Tighten the nuts using a ratchet wrench.

5. Cut the top of the legs flush with the top of the A-frame and truss brackets using a reciprocating saw.

6. Repeat steps 1 through 5 to build another A-frame. Build a third one with an A-frame bracket on both sides of the leg assembly.

Step B: Prepare the Swing Beam

1. On the 4 × 6 beam, mark the locations for the swing hangers. From the end of the beam, mark the bottom of the beam at 18", 36", 50", 68", 82", and 100".

2. Drill a 5⁄16" hole at each of the marks, centered from front to back. Insert a 5⁄16 × 7" swing hanger unit into each hole so the nailing plate covers the hook at the end of the hanger. Fasten a washer and nut on the end of each bolt using a ratchet wrench. Attach the nailing plate to the beam using 8d galvanized nails.

3. Measuring from the same end of the beam as in step 1, make a mark for the middle leg assembly at 110½" and 114". Make a mark on the face of the beam at 121½", 137½", and 153½" for the climbing wall.

4. Drill ¼" holes at the marks for the climbing wall 2" from the bottom edge of the beam. Insert ¼ × 4" eye bolts through the holes and fasten them with washers and nuts.

A. *Insert carriage bolts through the brace and legs. Fasten a washer and nut in the recesses, then tighten the nut.*

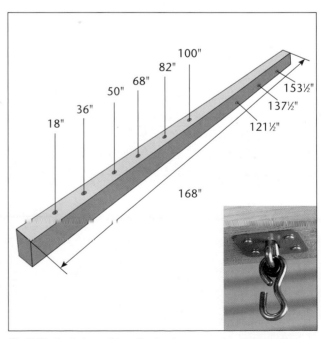

B. *Drill pilot holes and install swing hangers and eye bolts on the beam at the proper locations.*

Step C: Assemble the Structure

1. Drive two fence stakes in the ground 164" apart at the location you want to place the swing set. Stand an A-frame leg assembly with truss bracket in front of a stake (this is the swing set end) and the leg assembly with A-frame brackets on both sides in front of the other stake (this is the climbing wall end). Make sure the A-frames are level. The leg assemblies should be parallel with each other. Tie the assemblies to the stakes using thick string or wire.

2. Place the beam on top of the brackets on the leg assemblies. Center the beam so the ends overhang the outsides of the leg assemblies by 3½".

3. Fasten the beam in place by drilling pilot holes through the truss bracket and A-frame brackets and inserting ¼ × 2" lag screws.

4. Place the remaining leg assembly between the 110½" and 114" marks so the truss bracket faces the swing set side. Drill pilot holes through the truss bracket and insert ¼ × 2" lag screws.

5. Measure from one end of the climbing wall base and make a mark at 11", 21½", 32", and 43". Drill a ¾" hole at each mark, centered from top to bottom. **Note:** The climbing wall has three connections at the top, but four at the bottom.

6. Clamp the climbing wall base to the bottom front of the two legs that sit on either side of the climbing wall. Align the base with the bottoms and the sides of the legs. Drill two ⅜" holes at both ends of the base through the legs, staggering the holes. Drill all the way through the legs. Insert a ⅜ × 6" galvanized carriage bolt through each hole and tighten a washer and nut on the end of each bolt.

Step D: Attach the Accessories

1. Attach the swings and gym rings to the swing hangers, adjusting the chains so the accessories are level and at a proper height. Once the swings and gym rings are in place, use pliers to crimp the S-hooks on the hangers closed.

2. Attach the top of the climbing net to the eye bolts on the beams. Fasten the bottom of the net to the climbing wall base by inserting the loose ends of the rope through the holes in the base, pulling the rope tight, then tying the ends in knots.

Step E: Anchor the Structure

1. Fasten an anchor bracket approximately 2" from the bottom of a leg using the screw that came with the bracket.

2. Drive the auger anchor into the ground an appropriate distance from the bracket. Once the anchor is firmly planted in the ground, connect it to the anchor bracket. Do this for all six legs to help ground the structure.

C. *Tie the leg assemblies to fence stakes, then center the beam on the brackets and fasten it in place.*

D. *Attach the swings, gym rings, and climbing wall to the hangers and eye bolts.*

E. *Fasten anchors to the legs of the structure to keep them from moving.*

Small Play Projects

Small, portable projects are a great way to round out your backyard playground. Unlike the structures in the previous section, these items can be easily moved around your yard.

The projects explained in this section are relatively small, easy to build, and can provide hours of fun for your children. They require a minimal amount of space, so regardless of the size of your yard, you'll have room for most, if not all, of these projects.

Playground Accessories

Your children don't need massive play equipment to have fun. Small, simple play items can keep them entertained and challenged just as well as any large structures. A well thought out backyard playground will include a mix of both large and small projects to accommodate a wide range of children's interests.

The small projects covered in this section make ideal accessories for your backyard play area, and most of them can be brought indoors during the winter months so they can be enjoyed year round. They are designed to meet the diverse and changing needs of children.

The putting green and balance beam test their physical aptitude. The porch swing and picnic table provide a social setting for kids to sit down and talk, play, or eat. The sandbox fosters their sense of imagination as they play, create, and pretend. The plant and garden projects and the wildlife projects encourage their intellectual and learning abilities.

Likewise, the projects appeal to children of different ages. The swing and picnic table are designed for younger children. Older kids would probably not find the small structure comfortable, yet they might enjoy the opportunity to grow their own plants or flowers in the planter box. Other projects, such as the bird houses and observations station, appeal to all kids as they learn about wildlife.

The projects are safe for children to use and play with. By rounding corners, sanding the wood, and applying a paint or sealer to the finished product, there's little chance of kids ending up with splinters. These are also projects children can easily use without a lot of supervision.

You can have a lot of fun decorating these projects. The birdhouses on pages 114 to 115 are a great example of what you can accomplish with some creativity. These exciting finishes enhance the fun your kids will have with their projects. Children can even help with the decorating and painting.

A nice aspect of these projects is that they are simple to build. Most can be constructed in a matter of hours so there's not a big time commitment on your part. In addition, the cost of materials is relatively small, especially when compared to large play structures, so they're easy on the wallet.

Tools & Materials

Jig saw
Belt sander
Circular saw
Drill with ⅛" and ⅝" bits
Exterior wood glue
2½" galvanized screws
¼ × 3" lag screws (2)
5⁄16 × 6" lag eye screw (4)
Heavy chains (2)
2" chain connectors (6)
2 × 4 × 96" cedar (1)
2 × 6 × 96" cedar (1)
1 × 2 × 120" cedar (10)

Kid-sized Porch Swing

Your children will cherish the memories of spending pleasant summer days on their very own porch swing. This swing is about three-quarters of the size of a full-sized porch swing and is designed specifically for children. The gentle curves of the slatted seat and back are built for their comfort.

You can hang the swing from your porch, a tree branch, or under a deck. Be sure to balance the swing by properly adjusting the links on the chain. This particular swing was built with cedar lumber, which is long-lasting and attractive.

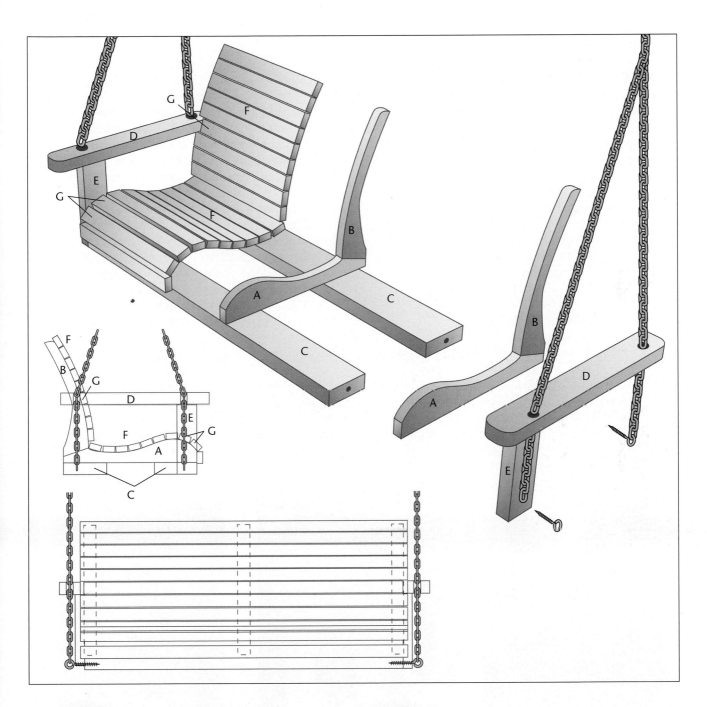

CUTTING LIST

Key	Part	No.	Lumber	Size
A	Seat Support	3	2 × 6	17½" (See template)
B	Back Support	3	2 × 6	14½" (See template)
C	Support Rail	2	2 × 4	39"
D	Arm	2	2 × 6	19 × 2⅝" (See template)
E	Arm Upright	2	2 × 6	8¾ × 2⅝"
F	Long Slats	17	1 × 2	40"
G	Short Slats	3	1 × 2	39"

HOW TO BUILD A PORCH SWING

Step A: Build the Seat & Back Supports

1. Enlarge the seat support and back support templates on page 107 using the grid system or a photocopier.

2. Trace the patterns for three sets of seat and back supports onto a 2 × 6, then cut out the pieces using a jig saw. Sand the edges smooth using a belt sander.

3. Apply wood glue to the flat section on the top of the seat support. Position the back support on top of the seat support, making sure the two pieces are flush at the inside corner, and clamp. Drill two ³⁄₁₆" pilot holes, then attach the two pieces using 2½" galvanized screws. Repeat this process for each seat-back support set.

Step B: Attach the Support Rails

1. Cut two 2 × 4 support rails at 39".

2. Set the joined seat and back supports face down on the edge of your work surface so the back support sections hang off the edge. Place a 2 × 4 support rail across the seat supports. Align the end of the rail with the outside and back edges of a side seat support. Drill two pilot holes in the support rail, then attach it using 2½" galvanized screws. Attach the rail to the other side seat support the same way.

3. Align the second support rail along the front edge of the seat supports, making sure the edges are flush. Drill pilot holes and attach the rail to the two outside seat supports using 2½" galvanized screws.

4. Center the third seat support between the side seat supports and attach it to the front and rear rails using two 2½" galvanized screws through each rail.

Step C: Build & Attach the Arms

1. Cut an arm at 19" and an arm upright at 8¾" from 2 × 6 lumber. Rip the boards down the middle to create two sets of arms and uprights about 2⅝" wide. Round the corners of the arms using a jig saw or a belt sander. Sand all the edges smooth.

2. Align the edge of an arm upright with the front edge of the front support rail. Make sure the upright is plumb, then drill two pilot holes and attach it to the support rail using 2½" galvanized screws.

3. Position the arm on top of the upright so it is flush with the inside of the upright and overhangs the front by 1½". Drill two pilot holes, then attach the arm to the upright using 2½" galvanized screws.

4. Make sure the arm is level, then drill a ⅛" pilot hole through the back support into the arm. Attach the arm to the back support using a ¼ × 3" lag

A. *Make sure the inside corner is flush, then attach each seat support to a back support with glue and galvanized screws.*

B. *Attach support rails to the seat supports using galvanized screws.*

C. *Drill a hole through the back support into the arm and attach it with a lag screw.*

screw. Repeat steps 2 through 4 for the other arm and upright.

Step D: Cut & Attach the Slats

1. Cut seventeen long seat slats at 40" and three short slates at 39" from 1 × 2 lumber.

2. Paint or stain the swing and the slats as desired. Allow the paint 24 hours to dry before continuing.

3. Install the long slats, beginning at the crook of the seat, spacing them evenly. Drill pilot holes, then attach each slat using a 1¼" galvanized screw driven into each seat support.

4. Install the short slats between the arms by driving a 1¼" galvanized screw into each seat support.

Step E: Drill Holes & Hang the Swing

1. Measure and make a mark on top of the arm 3" from the front edge and ¾" from the outside edge for the front chain hole. Make a mark for the rear chain hole at 1½" from the back edge and centered from side to side. Drill holes through the marked points using a ¾" spade bit.

2. Drill pilot holes and insert screw eyes into the ends of the rear support rail and ¾" from the bottom of the arm uprights.

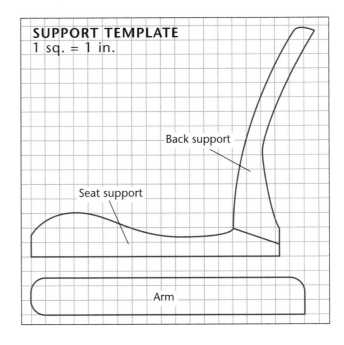

SUPPORT TEMPLATE
1 sq. = 1 in.

Back support

Seat support

Arm

3. Insert the chain through the arm holes and hook the chain to the screw eyes using chain connectors. Suspend the swing and adjust the length of the chain and the position of the connectors until the swing balances properly.

4. Hang the swing using heavy screw eyes inserted into ceiling joists or into a 2 × 4 lag-screwed across the ceiling joists.

D. *Install the finished slats, started at the crook and covering the seat and back. Space the slats evenly.*

E. *Suspend the swing and adjust the chain length and the position of the connectors until the swing balances.*

Tools & Materials

Circular saw
Drill with ⅜" and 1" bits
Tape measure
Saw protractor
Clamps
Finish sander
Rachet wrench
2 × 4 × 72" cedar (2)
2 × 6 × 72" cedar (5)
2 × 8 × 96" cedar (3)
2½" deck screws (32)
⅜ × 3" carriage bolts
with nuts and washers (16)

Children's Picnic Table

A picnic table is a wonderful addition to any backyard. Like other projects in this section, the children's picnic table is built at the right size for kids. Its light weight allows you to move the table around the yard for impromptu tea parties on the deck or dinner under the trees.

HOW TO BUILD A PICNIC TABLE

Step A: Cut the Lumber to Size

1. Use a saw protractor to mark a 50° angle on one end of a 2 × 6 leg. Cut the angle using a circular saw. Measure 32" from the tip of the angle, then mark and cut another 50° angle parallel to the first. Do this for all four legs, cutting two legs from one piece of lumber.

2. Cut two 48" seats and four 48" tabletop boards from 2 × 8 cedar.

3. Cut two 2 × 4 tabletop supports at 29¾". Measure 1½" from each end of both supports, make a mark, and cut a 45° angle. Cut a 2 × 4 tabletop board at 48".

4. Cut two 2 × 6 seat supports at 60". Measure 2½" from the ends of both supports, make a mark, and cut a 45° angle. Cut one 2 × 6 brace support at 30".

Step B: Assemble the A-Frame

1. Place one of the legs against the tabletop support so the inside edge of the leg is at the centerpoint of the support. Align the top of the leg with the top of the support. Clamp the pieces together.

2. Drill two ⅜" holes through the leg and support. Stagger the holes. Countersink 1" holes about ½" deep into the leg using the ⅜" holes as a guide. **Note:** If your washers are larger than 1", you'll need a larger recess. Insert a ⅜ × 3" carriage bolt into each hole. Tighten a washer and nut on the end of the bolt using a ratchet wrench. Repeat these steps to fasten the second leg in place.

3. Measure along the inside edge of each leg and make a mark 12½" from the bottom. Center the seat support over the leg assembly, on the same side of the legs as the tabletop support, with the 45° cuts facing down and the bottom flush with the 12½" marks. Drill ⅜" holes, countersink 1" holes, and fasten the seat support to the legs using carriage bolts.

4. Repeat Step B to assemble the second A-frame.

Step C: Attach the Table Top & Seats

1. Stand one of the A-frames upright. Place a 2 × 8 × 48" seat on the seat support so the seat overhangs the outside of the support by 7½". Align the back edge of the seat with the end of the support. Drill two 3⁄32" pilot holes through the seat into the support, then insert 2½" deck screws. Attach the seat to the second A-frame the same way. Fasten the seat to the other side of the table using the same method.

2. Center the 2 × 6 × 30" brace between the leg supports, making sure they're flush at the bottom. Drill two 3⁄32" pilot holes through the supports on each side, then fasten the brace to the supports using 2½" deck screws.

3. Place the 2 × 4 tabletop board across the center of the tabletop supports, overhanging the supports by 7½". Drill two 3⁄32" pilot holes on both ends of the top board where it crosses the supports. Attach it to the supports with 2½" deck screws.

4. Place a 2 × 8 top board on the table, keeping a ¼" gap from the 2 × 4. Drill pilot holes in the end of the board, then insert 2½" deck screws. Install the remaining top boards the same way, spacing them evenly with a ¼" gap. Allow the outside boards to overhang the end of the tabletop supports.

5. Sand any rough surfaces and splinters, and round over edges on the seat and tabletop, using 220-grit sandpaper.

6. Apply a stain, sealer, or paint following manufacturer's instructions.

A. *Use a saw protractor to mark a 50° angle on the end of the table leg, then cut the angle using a circular saw.*

B. *Fasten the tabletop and seat supports to the legs with carriage bolts. The nuts are recessed to prevent injury.*

C. *Install the 2 × 4 top board by drilling pilot holes and inserting deck screws, then install the 2 × 8 boards.*

Tools & Materials

Tape Measure
Circular saw
Drill with ⅛" and ½" bits
1⅛" spade bit
Router with ¾" dado bit
1½" galvanized screws
3" swivel caster wheels (2)
3" rigid caster wheels (2)
¼ × 1" lag screws
Landscape fabric
Rope, 36"
Exterior wood glue
220-grit sandpaper
1 × 10 × 48" cedar (1)
1 × 8 × 72" cedar (1)
1 × 2 × 96" cedar (3)

Rolling Garden

This garden on wheels is sure to be a favorite with your children. The unique design features dividers in the cart so kids can plant different flowers and vegetables or leave one section empty for carrying their watering can or other treasures. The back of the cart contains a tool caddy so children can take their gardening tools with them wherever they go. The 3" caster wheels make the cart easy to pull, and the swivel wheels in the front allow the cart to turn smoothly without tipping over.

HOW TO BUILD A ROLLING GARDEN

Step A: Prepare the End Panels

1. Cut two 1 × 10 end panels at 14" using a circular saw.
2. Make a mark 2¾" from the top along an edge of an end panel for the corner angle. Make another mark 4" from that edge along the top of the panel. Connect the two points using a straightedge. Repeat for the other corner.
3. Mark a horizontal line across the panel 1½" from the top edge. Measure 6" from each side and mark cross points on the horizontal line.
4. Set the two end panels together, making sure the edges are flush, and clamp them to your work surface. Drill holes for the handles using a 1⅛" spade bit centered on the cross points. Cut away the remaining material from the handle using a jig saw. Cut the corner angles using a jig saw. Sand all edges smooth using 220-grit sandpaper.

Step B: Build the Cart Frame & Dividers

1. Cut two 1 × 8 side panels at 24".

A. *Drill holes for the handles, then cut away the remaining material.*

2. To make grooves for the removable dividers, clamp the two side panels side by side on your work surface. Cut two ¾" wide × ⅜" deep dadoes in the side panels, 6" from each end, using a router and a straightedge guide.

3. Butt the panels together with the end panels over the side panels. Drill ⅛" pilot holes through the end into the side panels. Attach the side and end panels using glue and 1½" galvanized screws.

4. Cut a 1 × 10 divider at 12½". Rip the piece in half to form two 4½" dividers using a circular saw. Use a jig saw to cut a 1" wide × 1½" long notch in the bottom corners of each divider to fit around the support cleats.

Step C: Build the Cart Floor

1. Cut two 1 × 2 support cleats at 24" and two at 10½". Cut seven 1 × 2 floor slats at 24".

2. Make two marks on the inside of each side panel 1½" from the bottom edge. Align the bottom edge of a 24" support cleat along the marks and attach one to each side panel using 1½" galvanized screws spaced every 6-8".

3. Position the 10½" support cleats between the long cleats, making sure the edges are flush. Attach the cleats to the end panels with 1½" galvanized screws.

4. Turn the cart upside down and install the floor slats, leaving about ¼" of space between each slat to allow for drainage. Drill pilot holes through the ends

of the slats and attach them to the support cleats using 1½" galvanized screws.

Step D: Install the Tool Caddy & Finish Cart

1. Cut a 1 × 2 tool caddy floor at 10" and four dividers at 2½". Cut a 1 × 8 caddy wall at 10".

2. Assemble the pieces of the tool caddy, then fasten the pieces together by drilling pilot holes and inserting 1½" screws.

3. Position the caddy on the back end panel so the base is flush with the bottom edge of the cart. From inside the cart, drill pilot holes and insert screws into the two outer caddy dividers. Insert two additional screws from the underside of the cart into the caddy base.

4. Attach caster wheels to the floor slats, using ¼ × 1" lag screws. The wheels should be recessed inside the frame. For easy maneuvering, be sure to install swivel casters in the front of the cart.

5. Drill two ½" holes for the pull rope in the front panel, 3" from the side and 2" from the top. Thread a 36" piece of rope through the holes and knot the ends.

6. Line the bottom of the cart with landscape fabric and staple it along the panels. Insert dividers into the grooves to make separate growing or storage areas. Fill the cart with 6" of potting soil, then add seeds or plants.

B. *Cut dado grooves in the side panels for the removable divider walls.*

C. *Attach the floor slats to the support cleats with galvanized screws.*

D. *Assemble the tool caddy and attach it to the back end panel (top). Attach caster wheels so they are recessed inside the frame.*

111

Tools & Materials

Tape measure
Circular saw
Straightedge cutting guide
Finish sander
150-grit sandpaper
Miter saw
Drill and 1" bit
Hammer
4d galvanized finish nails
1¼" galvanized deck screws
⅝ × 48 × 96" fir siding
¾ × 24 × 48" CDX plywood
1 × 2 × 120" cedar (1)
1 × 4 × 96" cedar (2)

Planter Box

Planter boxes really spruce up your play area. You can paint or stain the boxes to match the play structures in your yard, and when they're bursting with flowers, they'll breathe life into the playground. Kids can have fun planting, watering, and watching flowers grow.

In addition to flowers, your children can also grow vegetables in these planter boxes. Carrots, radishes, and lettuce grow relatively quickly and make tasty treats when they reach maturity. Since the boxes are easy to build, make several to place at intervals to form borders along the edges of the playground.

HOW TO BUILD A PLANTER BOX

Step A: Cut & Assemble the Box Panels

1. Cut two 11⅛ × 22¼" side panels from fir siding using a circular saw and straightedge cutting guide. Cut two 11⅛ × 15" end panels from the same sheet of siding.

2. Clamp an end panel face down to the edge of your work surface. Butt a side panel against the end panel, face side out, flush at both ends. Drill ³⁄₃₂" pilot holes in the side panel every 4". Fasten the panels together using 1¼" deck screws. Add the second side panel to the end panel using the same process.

3. Set the remaining end panel face down on the work surface. Place the assembled pieces over the end panel to form a box, making sure the side panels are flush at the top and bottom with the end panel. Drill pilot holes every 4" and fasten the panels using deck screws.

A. *Butt a side panel against an end panel, drill pilot holes, then fasten them together with deck screws.*

Step B: Attach the Trim

1. Cut eight 1 × 4 corner trim pieces at 11⅛" using a circular saw.

2. Place a piece of corner trim on an end panel, aligning it with the top of the panel and the outside edge of the side panel. Attach the trim by driving 1¼" deck screws through the inside of the panel into the trim. Repeat this step to attach the trim on the other corners of the end panels.

3. Attach the corner trim to the side panels by butting the pieces of trim against the trim on the end panels. Align the side panel trim with the top and outside edge of the end panel trim. Fasten the trim in place by driving deck screws through the inside of the panels.

4. Drill three ³⁄₃₂" pilot holes in the overlapping corner trim pieces and fasten them together using 4d galvanized finish nails.

5. Cut two pieces of trim for the bottom of the side panels at 17" and two pieces for the end panels at 9¼". Place the bottom trim pieces between the corner trim, flush at the bottom, and fasten them in place using 1¼" screws driven through the inside of the panels.

Step C: Install the Bottom Panel

1. Cut two 1 × 2 cleats at 18" and two at 12". (The cleats do not run the entire length of the box.)

2. Place the cleats on the inside of the panels, making sure they are flush at the bottom, then fasten them in place using 1¼" deck screws.

3. Cut the bottom panel from CDX plywood at 15 × 21". Drill half a dozen 1" diameter holes in the bottom panel at staggered intervals.

4. Place the bottom panel on top of the cleats. The weight of the soil will hold the panel in place so it does not need to be nailed or screwed in place.

Step D: Cut & Attach the Mitered Cap Pieces

1. Cut two top caps from 1 × 2 cedar at 24⅝" and two at 18½". Once they're cut to length, use a miter saw to cut 45° miters on both ends of all four cap pieces.

2. Place the top caps on the box, aligning the inside edge of the caps with the inside of the panels. Make sure the corners are square and fit tightly together, then attach the top caps to the box using 4d nails.

3. Sand any rough areas with a finish sander and 150-grit sandpaper. Wipe away any dust and apply your choice of finish.

B. *Drive screws through the inside of the panels to attach the corner trim pieces.*

C. *Fasten the cleats at the bottom of the panels, then set the bottom panel on the cleats.*

D. *Cut 45° miters on the ends of the cap pieces, then attach them to the box using 4d galvanized finish nails.*

Tool & Materials

Tape measure
Drill and ¹⁄₁₆" bit
Spade bit
Jig saw or circular saw
Carpenter's square
Hammer
1 × 6 × 48" redwood or cedar
4d galvanized finish nails
Exterior wood glue
Shoulder hook

Bird Houses

You can embellish this basic birdhouse many ways, as in the examples below. There are, however, a few important things to keep in mind: don't paint or apply preservatives to the inside of the house, the inside edge of the entrance hole, or within ¼" of the face of the entrance hole or it will keep away the birds. The birdhouse can be hung with simple eyescrews and a chain, mounted on a post, or vertically mounted to a tree or other structure.

HOW TO BUILD A BIRDHOUSE

Step A: Cut the House Pieces

1. Cut the pieces of the birdhouse from 1 × 6 lumber following the cutting list on the opposite page.

2. On the front and back pieces, make a mark on each side, 2¾" from the top. Mark the center point at the top. Mark lines from the center point to each side, then cut along them.

3. On the bottom piece, make a diagonal cut across each corner, ½" from the end, to allow for drainage.

Step B: Drill the Entrance Hole & Score Grip Lines

1. Mark a point on the front piece 6¾" from the peak, centering the mark from side to side. Use an appropriately-sized spade bit to drill an entrance hole, usually 1¼ to 1½".

2. Use a wood screw or awl to make several deep horizontal scratches on the inside of the front piece, starting 1" below the entrance hole. (These grip lines help young birds hold on as they climb up to the entrance hole.)

Step C: Attach the Bottom

1. Apply wood glue to one edge of the bottom piece. Butt a side piece against the bottom piece so the bottoms of the two pieces are flush.

2. Drill ¹⁄₁₆" pilot holes and attach the pieces using 4d galvanized finish nails. Repeat this process for the front and back pieces, aligning the edges with the side piece.

Step D: Install the Pivoting Side

Set the remaining side piece in place, but do not glue it. To attach the side to the front and back pieces, drive a 4d nail through the front wall and another through the back wall, each positioned about ⅝" from the top edge. This arrangement allows the piece to pivot.

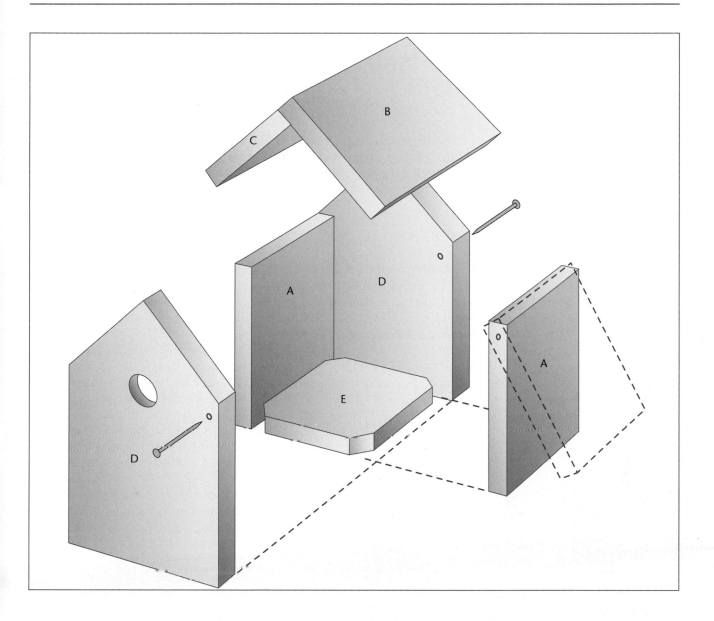

Step E: Add the Roof

1. Apply glue to the top edges of one side of the front and back pieces. Set the smaller roof piece on the house so its upper edge is aligned with the peak of the house.

2. Apply glue to the top edges on the opposite side of the front and back pieces. Place the larger roof piece in position. Drill pilot holes and drive 4d nails through the roof into the front piece and then the back.

Step F: Add the Finishing Touches

1. Drill a pilot hole in the edge of the front piece on the pivot wall side, placed about 1" from the bottom edge of the house. Screw in a shoulder hook, positioning it to hold the side piece closed.

2. Sand the birdhouse smooth, then paint or decorate it as desired. We hot-glued sticks and straw to the bird houses on the opposite page to create a "Three Little Pigs" theme. A brick exterior is painted on the third bird house and the roof is hot-glued into place.

CUTTING LIST			
Key	Part	No.	Size
A	Side	2	1 × 4 × 5½"
B	Roof	1	1 × 5½ × 6½"
C	Roof	1	1 × 4¾ × 6½"
D	Front/Back	2	1 × 5½ × 8¾"
E	Bottom	1	1 × 4 × 4"

Tool & Materials

Tape measure
Circular saw
Drill
Stapler
Tin snips
220-grit sand paper
Handle
Hinges (2)
2½" deck screws
1¼" deck screws
Brad nails
2 × 2 × 120" cedar (3)
½" CDX plywood
¼ × 1⅛" molding
Aluminum screen

Observation Station

An observation station allows children to safely observe bugs, insects, and wildlife in their own backyard. If the station will be used primarily for caterpillars, fireflies, grasshoppers, and butterflies, use a dense screen so they won't escape. For snakes, turtles, and frogs, a stronger screen with larger holes is appropriate.

HOW TO BUILD AN OBSERVATION STATION

Step A: Prepare Rails & Assemble the Frame

1. Cut two 2 × 2 rails at 24", seven rails at 21", six rails at 20½", four rails at 12", and two rails at 10½". Lightly sand any rough areas using 220-grit sandpaper. Wipe away any dust, then stain or paint the wood. Wait until the stain or paint is completely dry before continuing.

2. Butt a 21" rail against the inside edge of a 24" rail. With the top and the ends of the rails flush, drill two ³⁄₃₂" pilot holes into the rail. Attach the rails using 2½" deck screws. Fasten the second 24" rail on the outside of the opposite end of the 21" rail by drilling pilot holes and using deck screws. Fasten a 21" rail between the 24" rails at the open end to complete the base.

3. Place the rail assembly on its side and fasten a 20½" rail at each corner, making sure the edges are flush. Drill pilot holes and use deck screws to fasten the corners in place.

4. Measure 9" from the inside of a corner on the base and mark the rail. Attach a 20½" rail outside the

A. *Fasten the rails together by drilling pilot holes and inserting 2½" deck screws.*

mark, aligning the outside edges of the rail and the frame. Attach another 20½" rail on the opposite side of the frame at the same location.

5. Return the frame to an upright position. Place a 12" rail over one of the side rails installed in the last step, making sure it's flush on the side and end. Drill pilot holes and insert 2½" deck screws. Fasten the other end of the 12" rail to the corner rail. Secure a 12" rail on the opposite side by drilling pilot holes and using deck screws.

6. Place a 21" rail between the ends of the 12" rails. Align the 21" rail with the top and outside corners of the smaller rails, drill pilot holes, and insert deck screws.

7. Fasten the two 10½" rails on the inside edges of the two front corner rails, flush at the top and side. Fasten the other end of the 10½" rails to the side rails, 1½" from the top. **Note:** the 10½" rails are 1½" lower than the 12" rails.

Step B: Attach the Lid & the Bottom

1. Fasten the remaining two 12" rails on the outside edges of the last two 21" rails. Align the edges. Drill pilot holes and insert deck screws.

2. Attach two hinges to the back of the lid using the screws that came with the hinges.

3. Place the lid on the observation station. Attach the other end of the hinges to the adjacent rail. When closed, the lid should sit securely on the two front corners and the 10½" rails.

4. Cut the ½" CDX plywood to 24 × 24". Turn the station on its side and fasten the plywood to the bottom rails using 1¼" deck screws. The plywood should be flush with all four corners of the station. If it's not, adjust the box so it's square before fastening the screws.

Step C: Fasten the Screen to the Box

1. Cut the aluminum screen to size using wire cutters. Cut four screens at 22½ × 22½" for the sides and two screens at 10½ × 22½" for the top and lid.

2. Place each section of screen on the outside of the rails, overlapping each rail by ¾". Make sure the screen is flat against the rails. Staple the screen to the rails every 2".

Step D: Attach the Handle & Trim

1. Center a handle on the face of the front rail of the lid and attach it using the screws that came with the handle.

2. Cut a piece of ¼" × 1⅛" molding at 24" and place it along a rail on one side of the observation station. Align the molding with the end and outside edge of the rail, covering the screen, and fasten it to the rail using brad nails.

3. Measure the distance between the inside edge of the molding and the opposite corner. Cut a piece of trim to that size, then nail it in place. Do the same for the remaining two sides. Repeat to fasten trim to all sides of the observation station.

B. *Attach hinges to the lid and the frame.*

C. *Place the screen flat over the rails, then staple it every 2".*

D. *Cut pieces of trim to size, then nail them over the edges of the screen.*

Tools & Materials

Shovel
Reciprocating saw
Level
Drill with ³⁄₁₆" bit
Circular saw
Hammer
Utility knife
Miter saw
Coarse gravel
Sand
4 × 4 timbers
1 × 8 lumber
1 × 6 lumber
2 × 2 lumber
Wood sealer/protectant
Paint brush
Heavy duty plastic sheathing
2" galvanized screws
6" barn nails
Pavers
Rubber mallet

Timberframe Sandbox

A playground just isn't complete without a sandbox, and this version gives an old favorite a new look. It's much more refined than nailing four boards together and hoping for the best. The timber construction is not only charming, it's solid. A storage box at one end gives kids a convenient place to keep their toys. The other end has built-in seats, allowing children to sit above the sand as they play.

The gravel bed and plastic sheathing provide a nice base for the sandbox, allowing water to drain while keeping weeds from sprouting in the sand. The structure is set into the ground for stability and to keep the top of the pavers at ground level so you can easily mow around them. When your children outgrow the sandbox, turn it into a garden bed.

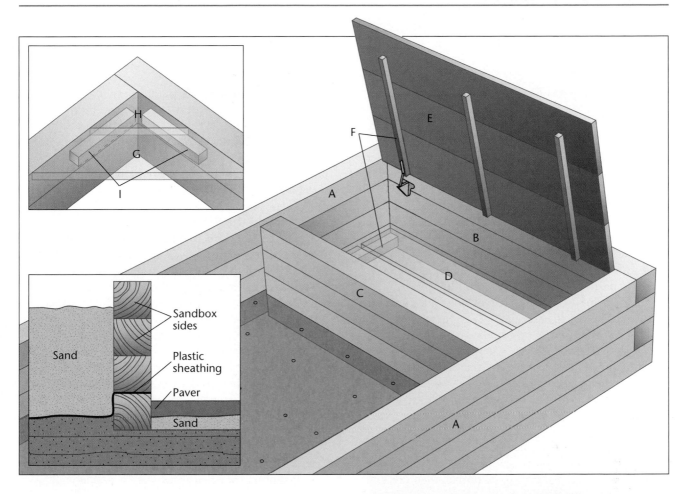

HOW TO BUILD A TIMBERFRAME SANDBOX

Step A: Prepare the Site

1. Outline a 48 × 96" area using stakes and strings.

Note: If you plan to install pavers (Step F), be sure to allow enough space for them around the sandbox.

2. Use a shovel to remove all of the grass inside the area. Dig a flat trench 2" deep by 4" wide around the perimeter of the area, just inside the stakes and string.

CUTTING LIST				
Key	Part	No.	Lumber	Size
A	Sandbox Sides	8	4 × 4	92½"
B	Sandbox Ends	8	4 × 4	44½"
C	Storage Box Wall	4	4 × 4	41"
D	Floor Boards	3	1 × 6	43"
E	Lid Boards	3	1 × 8	43½"
F	Floor & Lid Cleats	5	2 × 2	18"
G	Corner Bench Boards	2	1 × 6	18" w/ 45°angle
H	Corner Bench Boards	2	1 × 6	7" w/ 45°angle
I	Corner Bench Cleats	4	2 × 2	10"

A. *Use a shovel to remove the grass in the sandbox location, then dig a trench for the first row of timbers.*

119

Step B: Lay the First Row of Timbers

1. Cut the 4 × 4 timbers following the cutting list, using a reciprocating saw. Cut the rest of the lumber on the material list using a circular saw.

2. Coat all timbers and lumber with a wood sealer protectant. Let the sealer dry completely before continuing.

3. Place the first tier of sides and ends in the trench so the corners overlap. Position a level across a corner, then add or remove soil to level it. Level the other three corners the same way. Drill two ³⁄₁₆" pilot holes through the timbers at the corners, then drive 6" barn nails through the pilot holes.

4. Measuring from the inside of one end, mark for the inside edge of the storage box at 18" on both sides. Align the storage box timber with the marks, making sure the corners are square, then score the soil on either side of it. Remove the timber and dig a 3" deep trench at the score marks.

5. Replace the storage box timber in the trench. Its top edge must be ¾" lower than the top edge of the first tier of the sandbox wall. Add or remove dirt until the storage box timber is at the proper height.

6. Drill ³⁄₁₆" pilot holes through the sandbox sides into the ends of the storage box timber, then drive

6" barn nails through the pilot holes.

7. Pour a 2"-deep bed of coarse gravel into the sandbox section. (Do not pour gravel into the storage box area.) Rake the gravel smooth.

8. Cover the gravel bed section with heavy duty plastic sheathing. Pierce the plastic with an awl or screwdriver at 12" intervals to allow for drainage.

Step C: Build the Sandbox Frame

1. Set the second tier of timbers in place over the first tier and over the plastic sheathing, staggering the joints with the joint pattern in the first tier.

2. Starting at the ends of the timbers, drill ³⁄₁₆" pilot holes every 24", then drive 6" galvanized barn nails through the pilot holes. Repeat for the remaining tiers of timbers, staggering the joints.

3. Stack the remaining storage box timbers over the first one. Drill ³⁄₁₆" pilot holes through the sandbox sides into the ends of the storage box timbers, then drive 6" barn nails into the pilot holes.

4. Cut the excess plastic from around the outside of the sandbox timbers, using a utility knife.

Step D: Build & Install Storage Box Floor & Lid

1. Position a floor cleat against each side wall

B. *Lay the first row of timbers, including the wall for the storage box. Fill the sandbox area with a 2" layer of gravel and cover with plastic sheathing.*

C. *Build the rest of the sandbox frame, staggering the corner joints. Drill holes and drive barn nails through the holes.*

along the bottom of the storage box and attach them using 2" galvanized screws.

2. Place the floor boards over the cleats with a ½" gap between each board to allow for drainage. Fasten the floor boards to the cleats using 2" screws.

3. Place the lid pieces side by side on your work surface, making sure the ends are flush. Place three cleats across the lid, one at each end and one in the middle, making sure the end of each cleat is flush with the back edge of the lid. Drill pilot holes and attach the cleats using 2" galvanized screws driven through pilot holes.

4. Attach the lid to the sandbox frame using heavy-duty hinges and the included hardware. To prevent the lid from opening past a 90° angle or falling forward and causing injury, install an approved toy box lid support on the underside of the lid and the frame of the sandbox.

Step E: Build Corner Benches

1. To ensure the benches are flush with the top of the sandbox, make a mark ¾" down from the top edge of the sandbox at the corners. Align the top edge of the bench cleats with the mark and fasten them at the corners using 2" galvanized screws.

2. Wedge the smaller bench piece into the corner, resting on the cleats, then attach it using 2" screws. Butt the larger bench piece in place against the smaller piece, then attach it to the cleats. Repeat this step to install the second corner bench.

Step F: Fill Sandbox & Install Paver Border

1. Fill the sandbox section with sand to a depth of about 7".

2. Mark an area the width of your pavers around the perimeter of the sand box. Remove the grass and soil in the paver area to the depth of your pavers plus another 2", using a spade.

3. Spread a 2" layer of sand into the paver trench. Smooth the sand level using a flat board.

4. Place the pavers on top of the sand base, beginning at a corner of the sandbox. Use a level or a straightedge to make sure the pavers are even and flush with the surrounding soil. If necessary, add or remove sand to level the pavers. Set the pavers in the sand by tapping them with a rubber mallet.

5. Fill the gaps between the pavers with sand. Wet the sand lightly to help it settle. Add new sand as necessary until the gaps are filled.

D. *Attach the bench lid using heavy-duty hinges. Install a child-safe lid support to prevent the lid from falling shut.*

E. *Install 2 × 2 support cleats ¾" from the top of the sandbox. Attach the corner bench boards using galvanized screws.*

F. *Place the pavers into the sand base. Use a rubber mallet to set them in place.*

Tools & Materials

Circular saw
Drill
Tape measure
Router with ⅜" bit
Clamps
Framing square
Finish sander with 220-grit sandpaper
2½" galvanized screws
4 × 4 × 96" redwood beam
2 × 6 × 48" redwood lumber

Children's Balance Beam

HOW TO BUILD A BALANCE BEAM

Step A: Round & Sand the Beam

1. Round the top edges of the redwood beam using a router with a ⅜" rounding bit. Round both ends of the beam using a router.
2. Lightly sand the rounded edges using a finish sander and 220-grit sandpaper.
3. Sand the beam to remove any splinters.

Step B: Cut & Round the Base Supports

1. Measure and cut two 2 × 6 base supports at 24" using a circular saw.
2. Round the edges of the two base supports using a router.
3. Lightly sand the base supports.

Step C: Assemble the Beam

1. Position the beam on your work surface so the bottom is facing up.
2. Center the 24" base supports on the beam. Keep the edge of the supports 2" from the end of the beam. Make sure the supports are perpendicular to the beam using a framing square. Clamp the supports to the beam.
3. Drill three ³⁄₃₂" pilot holes in each base support. Stagger the holes to prevent splitting.
4. Fasten the supports to the beam using 2½" galvanized screws.
5. Sand out any rough spots using 220-grit sandpaper. Stain or paint the balance beam.

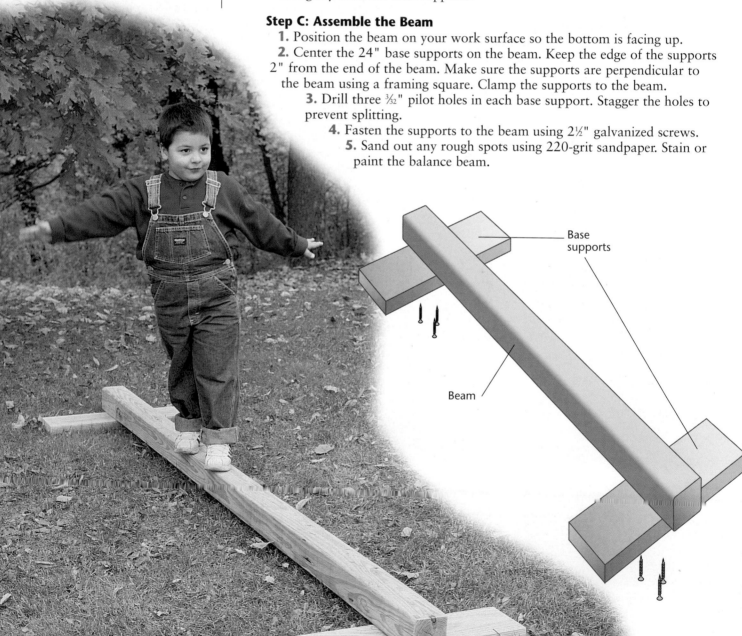

Base supports

Beam

Portable Putting Green

HOW TO BUILD A PUTTING GREEN

Step A: Cut the Sloped Base Supports
1. Cut four 1 × 2 base supports at 29".

2. Cut the slope on the first base support by first marking a point 9" from one end. Then draw a line from that point to the opposite corner at the end of the board. Cut the line using a jig saw. Use this board as a template to cut the other supports.

Step B: Build the Plywood Base
1. Cut the base at 20 × 30" and the ramp at 11 × 30" from ½" plywood, using a circular saw.

2. Position the supports across the bottom of the base. Align the two outside supports with the outside and back edges of the base and evenly space the other two supports about 9" apart. Drill counter-sunk pilot holes in the base, then attach the base to the supports using glue and 1¼" galvanized screws.

3. Sand one long edge of the ramp to a gentle bevel (approximately 15°) using a belt sander. Apply glue to the beveled edge of the ramp and the sloped edge of the supports. Butt the ramp against the edge of the base, then attach it to the supports using 1¼" screws driven through countersunk pilot holes. Don't worry if there is a slight gap between the base and ramp since the carpet will cover it.

4. Use a belt sander to bevel the leading edge of the ramp until it lies flat.

5. Cut two 1 × 4 side panels at 30½" and one back panel at 31½". Round one corner of each side panel using a belt sander. Attach the back and side panels to the base using 1¼" screws driven through pilot holes.

Step C: Install Cup & Carpet
1. Center the cup hole about 8" from the back wall. Trace the PVC end cap onto the plywood base at the hole location. Drill a starter hole to insert the blade of a jig saw, then cut out the hole. Attach the cup using hot glue.

2. Cut a 30" wide piece of indoor/outdoor carpeting using a utility knife. Attach the carpet to the base using double stick carpet tape and staples. Cut away the carpet over the hole.

Tools & Materials

Circular saw
Drill with countersink bit
Jig saw
Belt sander
Utility knife
Stapler and staples
Hot glue
Wood glue
Double stick carpet tape
3 × 12' indoor/outdoor carpet
1¼" galvanized screws
1 × 2 × 120" lumber
1 × 4 × 96" lumber
½" plywood
4" PVC pipe end cap

Carpet

Base

Ramp

Cup

Back panel

Side panel

Base supports

RESOURCES & CREDITS

Resources:
American Assoc. of Leisure and
Recreation (AALR)
1900 Association Drive
Reston, VA 20191
800-321-0789
www.aahperd.org/aalr/aalr.html

National Program for Playground
Safety School of HPELS
University of Northern Iowa
Cedar Falls, Iowa 50614
800-554-PLAY
www.uni.edu/playground

For copies of the *CPSC Handbook for Public Playground Safety* contact:
U.S. consumer Product Safety
Commission (CPSC)
Washington, DC 20207
800-638-2772
www.cpsc.gov

Contributors:
Hedstrom Corporation
www.hedstrom.com
800-934-3949

Weyerhaeuser
www.cedarone.com
866-233-2766
Structurally sound and naturally durable,
Weyerhaeuser's CEDARONE™ Timbers will stand
the test of time on outdoor playground structures.
CEDARONE's inherent natural preservative oils
means that the structure is free of toxic chemical
treatments and may be handled safely by children.

Wooden Whispers Play Systems
G.L. Huppert Enterprises, Inc.
1792 Ruth St.
Maplewood, MN 55109
651-779-8002
(Play structure and hardware kits)

Photographers:
Barbara Butler
San Francisco, CA
www.barbarabutler.com
©Barbara Butler: pp. 5, 22
©Teena Albert: pp. 12, 14-15, 22
©Michael Gilimanis p. 19

Gibson Stock Photos
Mt. Shasta, CA
www.markgibsonphoto.com
©Mark Gibson: p. 17

Index Stock Imagery, Inc.
New York, NY
www.indexstock.com
©Mark Gibson: p. 15
©Gareth Rockliffe: p. 17
©Bill Robbins: p. 18
©Jacque Denzer Parker: p. 26

NordicPhotos
Reykjakik, Iceland
www.nordicphoto.com
©NordicPhotos: p. 19

Illustrator:
Jan-Willem Boer/
Nancy Bacher-Artist Representative
Blaine, MN 55449
Jan-Willem Boer: pp. 25-26, 34,
44, 46, 49, 51, 53, 54, 66, 74, 89,
90-93, 95-97, 98

METRIC CONVERSION CHART

CONVERTING MEASUREMENTS

To Convert:	To:	Multiply by:
Inches	Millimeters	25.4
Inches	Centimeters	2.54
Feet	Meters	0.305
Yards	Meters	0.914
Square inches	Square centimeters	6.45
Square feet	Square meters	0.093
Square yards	Square meters	0.836
Cubic inches	Cubic centimeters	16.4
Cubic feet	Cubic meters	0.0283
Cubic yards	Cubic meters	0.765
Pounds	Kilograms	0.454
Millimeters	Inches	0.039
Centimeters	Inches	0.394
Meters	Feet	3.28
Meters	Yards	1.09
Square centimeters	Square inches	0.155
Square meters	Square feet	10.8
Square meters	Square yards	1.2
Cubic centimeters	Cubic inches	0.061
Cubic meters	Cubic feet	35.3
Cubic meters	Cubic yards	1.31
Kilograms	Pounds	2.2

LUMBER DIMENSIONS

Nominal - U.S.	Actual - U.S.	Metric
1 × 2	¾ × 1½"	19 × 38 mm
1 × 3	¾ × 2½"	19 × 64 mm
1 × 4	¾ × 3½"	19 × 89 mm
1 × 6	¾ × 5½"	19 × 140 mm
1 × 7	¾ × 6¼"	19 × 159 mm
1 × 8	¾ × 7¼"	19 × 184 mm
1 × 10	¾ × 9¼"	19 × 235 mm
1 × 12	¾ × 11¼"	19 × 286 mm
2 × 2	1½ × 1½"	38 × 38 mm
2 × 3	1½ × 2½"	38 × 64 mm
2 × 4	1½ × 3½"	38 × 89 mm
2 × 6	1½ × 5½"	38 × 140 mm
2 × 8	1½ × 7¼"	38 × 184 mm
2 × 10	1½ × 9¼"	38 × 235 mm
2 × 12	1½ × 11¼"	38 × 286 mm
4 × 4	3½ × 3½"	89 × 89 mm
4 × 6	3½ × 5½"	89 × 140 mm
6 × 6	5½ × 5½"	140 × 140 mm
8 × 8	7¼ × 7¼"	184 × 184 mm

INDEX

Also from

CREATIVE PUBLISHING INTERNATIONAL

Sheds, Gazebos & Outbuildings

*S*heds, Gazebos & Outbuildings delivers complete plans for 8 versatile buildings, including detailed step-by-step instructions with full-color photos and illustrations. Each project is adaptable to a variety of uses. Featured projects include a basic shed, lawn-tractor garage, timber-frame garden shed, victorian gazebo, playhouse, firewood shelter, garbage shed, and a lean-to tool bin.

ISBN 1-58923-008-6 . . . .$16.95

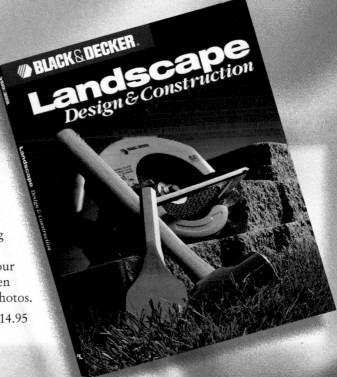

Landscape Design & Construction

*L*andscape Design & Construction guides you through landscaping your yard from the planning stages to the finishing touches. This perennial favorite includes a complete section on designing and planning your yard as well as in-depth instructions for more than a dozen popular projects, all illustrated by more than 400 color photos.

ISBN 0-86573-727-4 . . . .$14.95

CREATIVE PUBLISHING INTERNATIONAL

18705 LAKE DRIVE EAST
CHANHASSEN, MN 55317

WWW.CREATIVEPUB.COM